S0-BSA-802

THAT ONE FACE

THAT ONE FACE

STUDIES OF THE PLACE OF JESUS IN THE MINDS OF POETS AND PROPHETS

RICHARD ROBERTS

"That one Face, far from vanish, rather grows,
Or decomposes but to recompose,
Becomes my universe that feels and knows."
—ROBERT BROWNING

ASSOCIATION PRESS
NEW YORK: 347 MADISON AVENUE
1919

Copyright, 1919, by
The International Committee of
Young Men's Christian Associations

The Bible Text used in this volume is taken from the Revised Version of 1881.

CONTENTS

FOREWORD

It is hardly necessary to say that this is not in any sense a volume of literary estimates. It is simply an attempt to show "the face of Jesus Christ" as certain great souls have seen it; and nothing is added to this save what seemed necessary in order to provide the proper perspective.

The selection of those whose view of Jesus is treated in this book has been determined entirely by the fact that the present writer happens to have learned more from them than from any others. Obviously other lists of the same kind might be made by other men; but one may take leave to question whether the total result would be appreciably different.

Some of the contents of the following pages appeared in the author's book, "The Meaning of Christ," which was published in 1906, but has been for many years out of print. A few paragraphs of the twelfth week's material have been taken from the author's "The Renascence of Faith." All this matter has, however, been entirely rewritten.

CHAPTER I

Vision and Revelation

The aim of this book is to help men and women to reach a true judgment about Jesus. It does not pretend to provide all the conditions and materials of such a judgment. It will endeavor to set in order a certain *class* of material, in the hope that the reader may be stimulated to pursue the study further, and especially to consider afresh the portrait of Jesus in the gospels. To the gospel presentation of Jesus we shall naturally refer again and again in the course of the present study; but this will not do away with the need of a consecutive study of the gospels themselves. Indeed, this study will itself have proved a failure if it does not send those who may engage in it back to the gospels to seek out the face of Jesus for themselves.

It will be observed that what is proposed here is an endeavor to show how Jesus impressed certain persons. These persons are of two classes, poets and prophets. Of the company only one has an ecclesiastical connection of a formal kind, namely, Savonarola. The rest are all laymen; and consequently we may expect to find them largely free from professional and theological bias. The theological and clerical mind is perhaps open to the suspicion of partisan motives, of wanting to establish a case. The persons whom we propose to study will not suffer from this disadvantage. Indeed, some among them would have repudiated the suggestion that they ranked as orthodox Christians; one, Shelley, even called himself an atheist. It will at least be interesting to find out what these men thought about Jesus. What was it in Him that impressed them? How did they react to Him? Plainly this study should yield us some important material for a complete portrait of Jesus.

Perhaps, indeed, it may turn out that this is the most important material of all, outside the New Testament. There are in the creeds and confessions abundant definitions of the Person of Christ, but we have begun to recognize that formal statements of truth have grave limitations. Usually they have been fashioned in the fires of controversy; and consequently they overmuch reflect the bias of partisan views. But we also know nowadays that intellectual propositions cannot compass the whole meaning of life.

> "In divinity and love
> What's best worth saying can't be said,"

says Coventry Patmore in one of his poems; and this is particularly true of religious experience—most of all true of men's experience of Jesus. The touch of life is not in the creeds, in articles of faith deliberately and systematically drawn out. We are much more likely to find what we want in the spontaneous and often unguarded utterances of persons who simply spoke as they saw and were not in the least concerned to expound or to defend a particular view or tradition.

DAILY READINGS

First Week, First Day

Howbeit we speak wisdom among the perfect: yet a wisdom not of this world, nor of the rulers of this world, which are coming to nought: but we speak God's wisdom in a mystery, even the wisdom that hath been hidden, which God fore-ordained before the worlds unto our glory: which none of the rulers of this world knoweth: for had they known it, they would not have crucified the Lord of glory: but as it is written,

Things which eye saw not, and ear heard not,
And which entered not into the heart of man,
Whatsoever things God prepared for them that love
him.

But unto us God revealed them through the Spirit: for
the Spirit searcheth all things, yea, the deep things of
God. For who among men knoweth the things of a man,
save the spirit of the man, which is in him? even so
the things of God none knoweth, save the Spirit of God.
But we received, not the spirit of the world, but the
spirit which is of God; that we might know the things
that are freely given to us by God. Which things also
we speak, not in words which man's wisdom teacheth,
but which the Spirit teacheth; comparing spiritual things
with spiritual. Now the natural man receiveth not the
things of the Spirit of God: for they are foolishness
unto him; and he cannot know them, because they are
spiritually judged. But he that is spiritual judgeth all
things, and he himself is judged of no man. For who
hath known the mind of the Lord, that he should instruct
him? But we have the mind of Christ.—I Cor. 2: 6-16.

Our first business is to try to understand the peculiar
quality of the mind of the poet and the prophet.

William Blake once said that he saw not with his eyes
but *through* them; by which he meant that he saw *with*
his mind. To him, *seeing* consisted not in perceiving
alone, but in the way his mind reacted to the thing perceived. The vision included not only the object, but what
his mind was provoked to add to or to read into the object.
So he went on to say that when he looked at the sunrise, it was not a round disc of fire that he saw, but "a
great multitude of the heavenly host, crying 'Holy, Holy,
Holy, Lord God Almighty.'" So Francis Thompson looking at the sunset found in it a suggestion of his crucified
Lord: "Thou art," he sang,

"Thou art of Him a type memorial;
Like Him thou hang'st in dreadful pomp of blood
Upon thy western rood."

But it is given to few of us to see things after this

3

manner. This daring and flaming quality of imagination
is God's peculiar gift to the poet and the artist.

Yet great as this gift is, it is not God's greatest gift
of vision. For neither did William Blake at sunrise nor
Francis Thompson at sunset read in the face of the sun
its essential secret. They saw that God was there—
the one saw the Creator, the other the Redeemer; but
the image under which either saw Him was the creation
of his own imagination. Neither—as it were—saw
through the sun; what he did was to paint a picture on
the face of the sun, a picture essentially true no doubt,
but still a picture. The greatest gift of vision is not imagination but *insight,* not the gift that adds a picture,
however true, to the fact, but which pierces through the
fact and discovers the meaning hidden in its heart. This
same William Blake wrote a poem about the American
Revolutionary War; but for him the war-zone was not
the thirteen colonies, but the invisible no-man's-land between heaven and hell. He saw it not as a conflict of
men or of political interests, but as a struggle of titanic
spiritual powers. His fancy painted the war on a crowded
and bewildering canvas; but before his imagination had
got to work, his insight had perceived the issue to be one
of eternal principles. The war, as he saw it, was part
of the long and checkered drama of human liberation,
in which heaven and hell were as deeply engaged as
this world of living men. And this is the greater gift of
vision, that breaks through the crust of the outward
event to its core of spiritual reality. The poet must have
it if he is to be more than a minor poet; it is the first
necessity of the prophet. Some have a greater capacity
for it than others; but in his measure every man must
have it, for without it he goes through life blindfolded.

First Week, Second Day

**Howbeit when he, the Spirit of truth, is come, he shall
guide you into all the truth: for he shall not speak from**

4

himself; but what things soever he shall hear, these shall he speak: and he shall declare unto you the things that are to come. He shall glorify me: for he shall take of mine, and shall declare it unto you.—John 16: 13, 14.

What the true seer sees does not, however, depend solely upon his insight. Wordsworth in one of his poems asks,

> "Think you amid this mighty sum
> Of things forever speaking,
> That nothing of itself will come
> And we must still be seeking?"

Indeed, it is one of our commonest experiences that things do come to us. But in our day there has been considerable skepticism as to the value of anything that comes to us except along the accredited highway of the "scientific method." The only safe knowledge, we have been told, is that which we gain first through the senses and then through the exercise of reason upon the data gathered by our senses, the knowledge toward which we struggle by the exercise of our natural faculties. But from this view we are nowadays being gradually emancipated. While we accept the validity of the scientific method in its own field, we do not now believe that it is efficient over the whole field of possible knowledge.

"Reason," says G. J. Romanes, the English biologist, "is not the only attribute of man, nor is it the only faculty which he habitually uses in the ascertainment of truth. Moral and spiritual faculties are of no less importance in their respective spheres even of everyday life. Faith, trust, taste, etc., are as needful in ascertaining truth as to character, beauty, etc., as is reason. Indeed, we may take it that reason is concerned in ascertaining truth only where causation is concerned; the appropriate organs for its ascertainment where anything else is concerned belong to the moral and spiritual region."[1]

---

[1] "Thoughts on Religion," p. 112.

Henri Poincaré, in his book "Science and Method" tells how his discoveries in mathematics—and few men have made more or greater—*came* to him in sudden flashes. True, he had been seeking these things, but he did not arrive at them by process of conscious reasoning. They *arrived,* as it were, and often in irrelevant times and places, when his mind was engaged with other matters—all of which goes to show that while we have faculties that are essentially acquisitive, that go out and seek the truth, we have others the nature of which is receptive, they are there to receive such truth as may come to us; and both are essential to our knowledge of the truth.

Now Poincaré adds in his account of his experiences that these discoveries of which he speaks had been preceded by spells of intense mental concentration on the subject. He had gone out, as it were, resolutely to meet the truth, and then the truth had come to meet him. From this we may infer that no man will understand Jesus who does not put all the mind he has to the task. That, indeed, will not of itself bring a full understanding of Jesus; but without it there can be no understanding at all. Yet if a man will do this thing, the rest will come; and the process by which it comes we call revelation.

First Week, Third Day

Hear this word that the Lord hath spoken against you, O children of Israel, against the whole family which I brought up out of the land of Egypt, saying, You only have I known of all the families of the earth: therefore I will visit upon you all your iniquities. Shall two walk together, except they have agreed? Will a lion roar in the forest, when he hath no prey? will a young lion cry out of his den, if he have taken nothing? Can a bird fall in a snare upon the earth, where no gin is set for him? shall a snare spring up from the ground, and have taken nothing at all? Shall the trumpet be blown in a city, and the people not be afraid? shall evil befall a city, and the Lord hath not done it? Surely the Lord

God will do nothing, but he revealeth his secret unto his servants the prophets. The lion hath roared, who will not fear? the Lord God hath spoken, who can but prophesy?—Amos 3: 1-8.

The conditions of an adequate personal judgment upon Jesus—and indeed upon any subject that really matters —are *first,* insight backed by a concentrated effort of understanding; and *second,* revelation, a something communicated. The measure and vividness of a revelation depend upon the power and quality of one's insight; and that in its turn depends upon two things: *first,* natural endowment, and *second,* cultivation. The prophet is made by a unique original gift of insight, strengthened and sensitized by much thought and meditation, which make him capable of receiving great revelations. Prophets vary in size, of course. There are major prophets and minor, as there are major and minor poets.[2] But the difference between them is essentially one of scale and degree, not at all of kind. Moreover, it would be difficult to draw a psychological line which separates the prophet from the poet. The prophet is frequently a poet; and the poet is often a prophet. Both have the same quality of vision. The difference between them lies in another quarter, to which we shall attend presently.

Meantime, let us consider the nature of this *insight* more particularly. What we sometimes call "common sense" is a kind of insight. It consists of a sane perception of the relation of facts to each other, a just appreciation of their comparative importance, and a sound judgment upon the conduct proper to the situation. It is a useful and generous gift; and though we call it common, it is none too prodigally distributed. Few of us have as much as it would be good for us to have. Yet common

---

[2] In the Old Testament, the distinction between the major and minor prophets refers to the length of the books attributed to them. We are using the words here rather with reference to the quality of their message. The prophet who prophesies most is not necessarily the greatest prophet. Ezekiel is not a greater prophet than Amos.

sense operates only on the outside of things, and its peculiar danger is to assume that the things it is capable of dealing with cover the whole reality of life. But the greater part of life is, after all, out of sight; and we shall not reach a sound judgment concerning life until we have the power to penetrate its hidden regions—like Moses, to see the invisible. The distinctive quality of the prophet's and the poet's insight is that it is able to pierce this unknown and uncharted territory and to interpret life and man and God in the light of it. It is the gift of *spiritual* discernment and interpretation, the power to apprehend the spiritual reality which lies behind things and events, and to some extent to state the things seen in a language which others can understand. *To some extent,* notice; for all the spiritual reality which a man may perceive cannot be expressed in speech; it "breaks through language and escapes." As St. Paul says, we see only in part; and the part we see we only utter in part —whether we be prophets or poets, or only plain folk with a faint and flickering vision. But this is the distinction of the prophet and the poet—that they see things in this way. Peter Bell took "the primrose by the river's brim" at its face value; but the prophet and the poet see "every common bush aflame with God." For them reality lies not in things seen and temporal, but in the things which are unseen and eternal.

The difference between the poet and the prophet is simple. The poet sings; the prophet preaches. The poet clothes the thing he sees in a vesture of beauty and leaves it at that; but the prophet is forever trying to gain a hearing for his message. He has a truth to communicate to men; but he is not, as the poet is, concerned with the form in which the truth is uttered; his aim is to get it heard, anyhow and at any cost. By this it is not meant that the poet never preaches; on the contrary, every live poet preaches. But he does not *mean* to preach; and he preaches best when he least intends to. That is true of all art. All noble art communicates a truth; but it does so without meaning or professing to do so. But the prophet's business is the preaching. This, however, does not prevent him from being a poet; again and again prophecy has seemed to cast itself into poetic form. We see this in the Old Testament; and a notable instance of it is Lamennais' *"Paroles d'un Croyant,"* where the burning message of the prophet expresses itself in long rolling cadences like an ocean swell. The poet and the prophet are near neighbors.

First Week, Fourth Day

Now when Jesus came into the parts of Cæsarea Philippi, he asked his disciples, saying, Who do men say that the Son of man is? And they said, Some say John the Baptist; some, Elijah: and others, Jeremiah, or one of the prophets. He saith unto them, But who say ye that I am? And Simon Peter answered and said, Thou art the Christ, the Son of the living God. And Jesus answered and said unto him, Blessed art thou, Simon Bar-Jonah: for flesh and blood hath not revealed it unto thee, but my Father which is in heaven.—Matt. 16: 13-17.

This passage illustrates the difference between common sense and spiritual insight. When the ordinary man said Jesus was Elijah or Jeremiah or one of the prophets, he was expressing a judgment reached by common sense. So far as it went, it was true enough; and more, it was —in contrast with the prevailing official judgments—a favorable judgment. These people put Jesus in the highest class they knew, but it was a judgment arrived at by the exercise of natural faculty. They said that Jesus bore some family resemblance to the great figures of the prophetic tradition; but they failed to perceive the peculiar distinction of Jesus. It was left to Peter to see and to state what that was. *"Thou art the Christ of God."* But observe that Jesus explains Peter's perception of His significance by saying that he had received it from God. "Flesh and blood"—that is, natural faculty—"hath not

9

revealed it unto thee, but my Father which is in heaven."
Peter's judgment of Jesus was the product of spiritual
insight completed by a revelation.

The signal instance of this spiritual perception and
interpretation of Jesus is the Fourth Gospel. The Synoptic
Gospels in the main tell the story of Jesus in a plain
narrative without much comment; and record His teaching
as they found or received it. But the Fourth Gospel is
a spiritual interpretation of the story told by the synoptics.
It endeavors to see the figure of Jesus apart from its
historical setting; that is to say, it endeavors to place Him
in relation to the unseen world of eternal reality; and
its judgment is recorded in the Prologue of the first
chapter, where Jesus is identified with the *Logos,* the
Word, the eternal self-expression of God. Though the
Fourth Gospel is for the most part in narrative form,
it is deliberately placed in a setting which is curiously
timeless and careless of precise historical accuracy. Its
background is eternity.

The form of the Fourth Gospel's estimate of Jesus
was due to the intellectual background of the writer. The
term *Logos* may be said to begin its philosophical history
with Plato, who uses it to describe the eternal thought
of God, the perfect self-expression of God, as it were, in
its outgoing toward man. It was greatly developed in
Alexandria under Philo the Jew, who enriched the Greek
conception of the *Logos* by connecting it with the Wisdom
doctrine of the Jews, which broadly corresponds to the
Logos idea. But the Hebrew Wisdom was frequently
spoken of as a person, which at first may have been no
more than the common tendency to personify abstract
ideas, but which became more pronounced in Philo. It
is clear that, by some means or another, the teaching of
Philo had influenced early Christian thought. St. Paul
in the first chapter of Colossians shows undoubted traces
of it; as do the opening words of the Epistle to the
Hebrews. But this drift of thought receives its crowning

expression in the Prologue of the Fourth Gospel, where
the proposition is plainly set down that "The Word became flesh and dwelt among us"; and the view of the
Fourth Gospel is that the Word became flesh in the
Person of Jesus.

From this we may infer that what men see in Jesus is
influenced by their own mental background. It is this
that, partly at least, explains the wonderful diversity in
men's judgments upon Him; and that men see Him so
variously and so differently shows how unique a personality He was.

First Week, Fifth Day

Having therefore such a hope, we use great boldness
of speech, and are not as Moses, who put a veil upon his
face, that the children of Israel should not look stedfastly
on the end of that which was passing away: but their
minds were hardened: for until this very day at the reading of the old covenant the same veil remaineth unlifted;
which veil is done away in Christ. But unto this day,
whensoever Moses is read, a veil lieth upon their heart.
But whensoever it shall turn to the Lord, the veil is taken
away. Now the Lord is the Spirit: and where the Spirit
of the Lord is, there is liberty. But we all, with unveiled face reflecting as a mirror³ the glory of the Lord,
are transformed into the same image from glory to
glory, even as from the Lord the Spirit.—II Cor. 3: 12-18.

The peculiar value of the prophet's and the poet's vision
of Jesus lies in its spontaneity. Each from his own
angle and with his special gift of insight looks upon Him
and tells us what he sees. Very often he does not do so
intentionally; he does not set out to tell us what he sees.
The judgment is implied rather than deliberately stated;
and the richest clues are frequently those which are
dropped incidentally here and there. There is no suspicion
that someone is trying to prove a case or to defend an
opinion about Jesus. We have an unstrained reaction to

³ Margin, "beholding as in a mirror."

the personality of Jesus; and this should prove the best kind of material for a study of the significance of Jesus. We ought to find more truth about Jesus here than in the creeds. For the creeds are the records of intellectual findings. In our prophets and poets we shall find the verdict of life.

But when we speak of the spontaneity of the poet and the prophet, we must be careful to observe that their impression of Jesus was not received on a clean canvas. We have already observed that a man's view of Jesus is affected by his mental background. It has, however, to be noted that a man's mental background is composed of two elements—that which he has put into it himself by his own thought and self-discipline; and that which he has inherited. Sometimes what he has put in himself has largely obliterated what he found there when he began to look into it; sometimes his own contribution has been wholly determined by what was there before. But neither of these extremes describes the case of the great majority of men. Most of us endeavor to harmonize our inheritance with the things we subsequently learn. We are neither incorrigible conservatives nor incorrigible rebels.

When we speak of inheritance here, we are thinking not of any bias of physical heredity, but of what Mr. Benjamin Kidd calls "cultural" or "social heredity." It is not what is born in us that matters so much as what we are born into—the kind of atmosphere, whether religious, political, or social. It is that which seems chiefly to determine the *set* of our life. Dante, for instance, had a Catholic inheritance; and Browning was a product of English Protestant non-conformity; and neither ever outlived the mental habit which was imposed upon him by his native setting. It would be interesting to speculate what the result would have been if Dante and Browning could have brought their minds in a kind of virgin newness to the contemplation of Jesus; but that was no more

possible to them than it is to us. We have to acknowledge
that they approached Jesus with a certain inherited bias;
and for that we must make what allowance we can in
our study of them.

But there is an important distinction to be drawn here.
While we are inevitably children of our social and religious environment and never quite outgrow the kind of
mental habit which it induces in us, yet it does not follow
that we shall adhere to all the ideas and doctrines which
our fathers held. Dante inherited and retained a Catholic
habit of mind, but this did not prevent his repudiating a
part of the current Catholic teaching; Browning inherited
and retained a Protestant habit of mind, but he cannot be
cited as an orthodox Protestant. They exercised the right
to form independent personal judgments. They did not
accept their view of Jesus from the creeds; the view we
find in them is their own, and the fact that Dante's view
was that of a pious medieval Catholic does not alter this
fact. We have to do with the judgments of men who were
free to make up their own minds.

This raises a question for ourselves. Not one of us
has a right to take his view of Jesus ready-made. He
has to reach his own conclusion. The outlook and working of our minds are profoundly and in most cases permanently affected by the tradition we were born into. At
the same time we must not blindly accept the body of
doctrines and formulæ in which our fathers cast their
faith and their spiritual experience. For faith and experience, being living things, should also be growing
things; and they require to be continually embodied in
new forms and new statements more consistent with their
expanding life. So that it is not wrong to sit lightly
to past traditions. We must, of course, respect the past,
but we must not be bound by it. Tradition is a good thing
when it is kept in its proper place; but that place is
behind us and not ahead of us. And generally there is
as much of tradition embodied in the stuff of our minds

as we need, without our carrying over the formal system of doctrine in which it expressed itself. If we are to gain a personal impression of Jesus that is going to be our own, we must not start out with a fixed idea that a particular dogma concerning Him must be finally and forever true, as though the Spirit of God had no more to tell us about Him. We must approach Jesus freed from prejudice and preconception. This is what our prophets and poets did; they went out to explore His meaning without being bound by past interpretations of Him. And this is what St. Paul calls "beholding with unveiled face."

First Week, Sixth Day

But when the Comforter is come, whom I will send unto you from the Father, even the Spirit of truth, which proceedeth from the Father, he shall bear witness of me: and ye also bear witness, because ye have been with me from the beginning.—John 15:26, 27.

The book of Acts begins with the statement that Luke's gospel was a record of what Jesus *began* both to do and to teach; from which it is a fair inference that the writer believed that the Acts of the Apostles were a continuation of the deeds and words of Jesus. But if this means anything at all, it means that Jesus still continues to work in every enterprise and is present in every experience which is in line with the record of the Apostles' experience and teaching. And so it is fair to infer once more that men's experience of Christ after the days of the Apostles contains material which is necessary to an adequate judgment upon Jesus. It may be even asked whether we have not come to a better position to reach an understanding of Jesus than any previous generation since the days of the Apostles. The Apostles had one qualification for understanding Jesus which we have not and for the lack of which nothing can compensate us. They had lived with Him. But apart from that, we do know more about what Jesus has done and therefore are better placed for an understanding of Jesus than any who have gone before us.

This is borne out by the history of the creeds. The creeds were an attempt to capture the meaning of Jesus into a phrase. The attempt could not succeed in so far as it was meant to fix the doctrine concerning Jesus permanently. For one thing, words, being only symbols, cannot gather into themselves the whole reality of spiritual experience. Something is left out; and that the most important thing of all, the life itself. You cannot compress life into a form of words. It "breaks through language and escapes." But further, a form of words which may satisfy one generation cannot satisfy another, if the spiritual experience has gone on growing. And so the creeds have had to be patched up and extended, in order to try to include new apprehensions of truth contained in the growing experience. For instance, before it reached its present form in 740 A. D., the Apostles' Creed, between 150 A. D. and that year, had passed through at least twenty phases. The importance of the creeds is that they are landmarks in the history of the growth of human thought about Jesus. They have no finality; they register the general impression of Jesus in the age in which they were formulated. We stand on them, but we ought to go beyond them.

And, indeed, if our spiritual life is a reality we are bound to go beyond them. As Bradford the Puritan said—God has still more light and truth to break forth from His holy Word; and the Fourth Gospel suggests that there is more truth into which the Spirit of God is yet to guide us. The value of our prophets and poets in this connection is that we may learn from them how the Spirit of God is still testifying to men concerning Jesus; and it would require a good deal of hardihood to say that He has finished His work. Our study will show us something of the peculiar wealth of the personality of Jesus; and it will suggest to us that the treasure house is not yet exhausted. As we must be careful not to take our view of Jesus from the creeds, we must also avoid the danger of accepting the view of a prophet or a poet. We must take their views as materials with which to form our own; and if we seek a true vision in a spirit of eagerness and humility and diligence, it will not be denied to us.

First Week, Seventh Day

And he went out from thence; and he cometh into his own country; and his disciples follow him. And when the sabbath was come, he began to teach in the synagogue: and many hearing him were astonished, saying, Whence hath this man these things? and, What is the wisdom that is given unto this man, and what mean such mighty works wrought by his hands? Is not this the carpenter, the son of Mary, and brother of James, and Joses, and Judas, and Simon? and are not his sisters here with us? And they were offended in him.—Mark 6: 1-3.

But why is it so important that we should endeavor to reach a right personal judgment about Jesus? Why should He be singled out in this way from among so many great and notable figures in history, and one's attitude to Him be declared to be a matter of life and death?

Perhaps we can best answer this question by quoting another. Eucken, the German philosopher, speaking of the life of Jesus, asks: "How came it to pass that this particular point was the fountainhead of so mighty a movement, that old ideals were shattered, and new ones arose, that the whole previous balance of life was upset and previous standards failed to satisfy, that a mighty longing took possession of mankind, a stormy unrest which even now after hundreds of years is not allayed?"

The distinction between B. C. and A. D. is not merely an affair of the calendar. It represents a very important historical circumstance—namely, that a new quality entered into life when Jesus appeared in the world, which has profoundly affected the course of human affairs. Sup-

pose that useful person, the "man from Mars," were to
visit us and to examine our human story during the last
twenty centuries. He would find that it is dominated by
one figure. The greatest and oldest voluntary society
known to history is called by His name; many of the
most significant passages in secular history gather around
His person. Many of the greatest achievements of mankind in literature, art, and music either commemorate
Him or owe their inspiration to Him. Hardly a single
department of our life but has been touched and profoundly modified by Him. In short, it is impossible to
understand the history of two millenniums without reference to Him. He is by far the most outstanding figure in
the history of the world, and His influence upon the lives
and affairs of men is unique and without parallel. And
today, after so long a time, His name has power to evoke
from men large sacrifices and to inspire them to great
heroism.

But there is even more than this to be explained—
the unique impression He has consistently made upon the
minds of individual men. "You may go to the Nicene
Creed or the Formula of Chalcedon or the Augsburg Confession to see how men defined and placed the Person of
Christ; and you may think them right or wrong. But
what we have to reckon with is the circumstance that
hundreds and thousands of men and women in every
generation since His day have had a sense of His significance to their lives which they could express only by
worshiping him as God, that when they thought of God
they thought of Jesus, and that it was the face of Jesus
which they saw when they prayed to God." And this has
happened to no person in history in the permanent and
universal way in which it has happened to Jesus.

And the problem which has to be solved is this: This
person, who has gained this strange ascendancy over
men's minds and hearts, has so profoundly influenced their
history, was a peasant, born in an obscure village in an

obscure land, who lived his life in circumstances of consistent lowliness and quietness in an out-of-the-way corner
of the world, far from the highroads of its traffic, and
who died a malefactor's shameful death. It is, at least,
of some considerable importance to our outlook upon life
to try to understand how this strange reversal came about.
It surely has a good deal to tell us about the kind of
world we live in and the way in which we should relate
ourselves to it. Quite apart from the traditional teaching
of the Church about Jesus, the bare facts of the historical
consequences of His life and death and the total impression which He has made upon the minds of men through
the ages since His coming require that we should make
a serious effort to understand Him, even if it were only
for the sake of informing ourselves about a striking historical phenomenon.

SUGGESTIONS FOR THOUGHT AND DISCUSSION

Was the inspiration of the Old Testament prophets
different in kind from that of Savonarola? If so, in what
way?

Is it reasonable to suppose that revelation ceased when
the last book of the New Testament was written? If not,
in what quarters are we likely to find traces or records
of later revelations?

What is the proper relation between the *old* and the
new in thought? And what is the proper attitude to take
towards them? If the *old* is not to be accepted without
question, by what principles are we to judge it? How
are we to test the *new* in order that we may know that
it is true?

How far is it reasonable to believe that there is more
to be known about the significance of Jesus than is known?

CHAPTER II

A General Survey

We have already observed that if we could send a man who has no previous knowledge to examine the literature of the last twenty-five centuries, his strongest impression would be that, at a certain point, a personality altogether unique in wealth and power impinged on the life of man, gradually changing the tone and stress of literature and exerting a permanent influence on it. If that man were sent through a modern art gallery, where he might see some of the great masterpieces of painting, equally he would discover that the supreme interest has gathered around this same person, who is represented in an endless number of aspects, yet is always easily recognizable. The absolute preeminence of Jesus Christ in the essential art and literature of nineteen centuries is beyond serious question. He has had no competitor. At the same time it should be remarked that the growth of Jesus' influence upon Literature and Art has not been a constant quantity. There have been periods of strange sterility in both domains during the Christian era. For one period of a thousand years, indeed, Art has practically nothing, and Literature very little that is new to tell us of the significance of Jesus.

It was not that men did not think much of Jesus that the art and literature of that period say so little that is new concerning Him. That there was no such growth in men's understanding of Him during that period as in the three previous and the six subsequent centuries, seems to be due in the main to the tendency to place the Church at the center of interest rather than Jesus. It was the period of ecclesiasticism, of the elaboration of the Catholic idea and practice.

The story of how the Church came to be more concerned about its own place in the scheme of things than about its Lord's is a long one and can only be told very summarily here. It begins with the so-called "conversion" of Constantine early in the fourth century. At that time the Church became formally associated with the secular state; hitherto the Church had been free and independent; now it became an official corporation. And, as is the way with official corporations, it began to be more interested in its status than in its mission. Its history during the next eight or nine centuries was largely that of a struggle for supremacy with the State; and in the weapons it used, in the spirit it showed, there is little perceptible difference between it and the State. Its life became largely external; its conception of well-being was determined by the ordinary standards of the world. It became largely despiritualized and lost the open vision. And it is significant that the first conspicuous sign of a new apprehension of Jesus after this sterile period was in Dante, who was, as we shall see, also a vehement preacher of the doctrine of the separation of Church and State.

Yet during this period there were those who kept the flame of spirituality alive. The monastic movement was in its origin a protest against the spiritual bankruptcy of the official church; and in the desert, in caves of the rocks, in remote cloisters, men like Anthony, Augustine, Martin of Tours, Jerome, and Benedict of Nursa (the founder of the Benedictine Order) kept the altar-fires burning. And we may presume that there was always a succession of faithful souls, living obscure and unrecorded lives in the common ways of men, who passed on the living word in humility and sincerity from generation to generation. Professor Lindsay in his "History of the Reformation" has shown us that there was "a simple family religion in numberless German homes in the end

20

of the fifteenth century"; and this humble, social, religious life owed little to the prevailing ecclesiastical system. It is, indeed, in such byways of lowly piety and unpretentious saintliness that we are to seek the real channels by which the Christian life has come down the ages. In this period which we are now discussing, this living Christian hope does frequently break out through the surrounding darkness, as it did for instance in the English poet Cynewulf who sang of

"The great Leader, the Prince Majestic,"

who

" 'Twixt God and man placed a ghostly pledge of love."

This was in 800 A. D., about the midpoint of the sterile millennium. With Dante, however, we see beginning a new age of faith and spiritual insight; and our present task will deal with some of the figures of this later period. But it may be worth while to preface our study of the prophets and poets by a brief survey of the history of the treatment of Jesus in Art.

It is a matter of common knowledge that Art sought at a very early period to represent Jesus, here by a simple symbol, there by a more deliberate attempt at portraiture. Whether these early portraits of Jesus conveyed a real likeness of Him is doubtful. Sir Wyke Bayliss says they do; Dean Farrar denies it. But it really does not matter very much. One thing, however, is significant enough, namely, that from the beginning the painter put into his picture what is virtually a confession of failure to include in the portrait all that he knew ought to be there. Was not the aureole intended to symbolize something which the painter felt to be there, but which refused to submit to pencil or pigment?

But perhaps the most significant thing of all in the story of Christian art is the complete change which came over the conception of Jesus in Art after the lapse of the arid millennium. During that long period Art had simply reproduced the earlier tradition; but with the great awakening of modern enlightenment in the fourteenth century, there came a new race of painters, as fresh and prolific in their ideas as their immediate predecessors had been sterile and uninspired.

DAILY READINGS

Second Week, First Day

I am the good shepherd: the good shepherd layeth down his life for the sheep. He that is a hireling, and not a shepherd, whose own the sheep are not, beholdeth the wolf coming, and leaveth the sheep, and fleeth, and the wolf snatcheth them, and scattereth them: he fleeth because he is a hireling, and careth not for the sheep. I am the good shepherd; and I know mine own, and mine own know me, even as the Father knoweth me, and I know the Father; and I lay down my life for the sheep. And other sheep I have, which are not of this fold: them also I must bring, and they shall hear my voice; and they shall become one flock, one shepherd.—John 10: 11-16.

Christian art made the first faltering attempts to represent Jesus that still survive, in the Catacombs, in the second and third centuries, doubtless working upon a still older tradition. He is frequently represented as "the good Shepherd"—"a beautiful, graceful figure," as Dean Stanley has said. This fact is altogether suggestive of the freshness and bloom which the early Christians discerned in the world after the coming of Jesus. Before He came the world had grown old and gray and weary; the pallor of death was upon its face. Judaism was at its last gasp; Greek philosophy was no more than a ruin of its great past; Pan, great Pan, was sick unto death. But the coming of Jesus revitalized this old decadent world; and a new joy and light entered into it. The exuberance and spring of men newly regenerate in a world in which Hope had been raised from the dead, found

expression in the fresh joyful young Shepherd of the
Catacomb drawings. All this, mark, in the Catacombs,
where the young Church lay in hiding, where its martyrs
were laid to rest. So strong was the new hope that Jesus
had awakened that the gloom of the Catacombs, with all
their memorials of bitter persecution, failed to dispel it.
And on those walls it graved, in its drawings of Jesus,
a witness to its own faith and life which remains to
this day.

There is one characteristic of the Catacomb pictures
of the good Shepherd which has been often mentioned
and which is worth recalling here. In one of the doctrinal controversies in which the Church was involved,
the "fierce Tertullian" (A. D. 160-230) had asserted,
"The sheep He saves, the goats He does not save," and,
perhaps in conscious protest against the African Father's
severity, the artists of the Catacombs represented Jesus
as carrying on His shoulders not a lamb but a kid. "She
sighed," sang Matthew Arnold in one of his sonnets,

> "The infant Church! of love she felt the tide
> Stream on her from her Lord's yet recent grave.
> And then she smiled; and in the Catacombs,
> With eye suffused but heart inspired true,
> On those walls subterranean, where she hid
> Her head 'mid ignominy, death, and tombs,
> She her Good Shepherd's hasty image drew—
> And on his shoulders, not a lamb, a kid."

The mercy, the hope which were in Jesus—these were the
outstanding elements in the Christian experience of the
early centuries; and it was this that expressed itself in
the drawings on the Catacomb walls. That youthful,
joyous "good Shepherd" is an important contribution to
our understanding of Jesus.

Second Week, Second Day

And I turned to see the voice which spake with me.
And having turned I saw seven golden candlesticks; and

in the midst of the candlesticks one like unto a son of man, clothed with a garment down to the foot, and girt about at the breasts with a golden girdle. And his head and his hair were white as white wool, white as snow; and his eyes were as a flame of fire; and his feet like unto burnished brass, as if it had been refined in a furnace; and his voice as the voice of many waters. And he had in his right hand seven stars: and out of his mouth proceeded a sharp two-edged sword: and his countenance was as the sun shineth in his strength. And when I saw him, I fell at his feet as one dead. And he laid his right hand upon me, saying, Fear not; I am the first and the last, and the Living one; and I was dead, and behold, I am alive for evermore, and I have the keys of death and of Hades.—Rev. 1: 12-18.

Look now at the other end of that sterile middle period. "During the early and middle periods of Christian art," says Sir Wyke Bayliss, "we look in vain for *expression* on the face of Christ." It was this—*expression*—which the great painters of the Awakening added to the portraiture of Jesus. But does not this imply a deeper understanding of Jesus? The painter executes not the mere likeness of a man—the camera can do that—but

"So paints him that his face
The shape, the colour of a mind and life
Lives for his children, ever at its best."

In some respects the Renascence painters follow tradition, but in their own distinctive contribution to the portraiture of Jesus, it was this further thing indicated by Tennyson that they introduced.

The awakening began in the fourteenth century, and it gave us Dante, Petrarch, and Langland in Literature, as it began a new era in Christian art. Art, like Literature, had its morning stars; but the great dawn began with Giotto and Cimabue; then Fra Angelico in Italy and the van Eyck brothers in Flanders took up the tale, until we reach the great age of Michelangelo, Titian, Raphael,

Correggio, and da Vinci. "From this quintet," says one great authority, "have come the finest interpretations of the face of Christ the world has ever seen." And this happened because these men came to their work with a reverent insight borne on a surging new life. A friend who had come to see da Vinci's great picture "The Last Supper" remarked first of all the brilliancy of the silver cup; da Vinci took his brush and painted the cup out —he would have nothing in his picture which drew attention away from its central Figure. That was the spirit of the time within this particular region. Unfortunately, da Vinci's picture has all but perished; but the original sketch of the face of Jesus made for "The Last Supper" still exists. In that study, da Vinci has embodied in undying beauty the sad, tender grace which he read in the countenance of Jesus. And as da Vinci has given us a picture of the tender, gracious, comforting Jesus, so Michelangelo has in his "Dies Iræ" depicted Christ's hatred of the sin which rejects His grace. Raphael, in his picture of the Transfiguration, leads us into the secret places of Jesus' power, His intense communion with God; Titian, in his picture of the incident of the Tribute Money, has shown us the perfectly balanced, strong character, the quiet reserve of which only revealed its great strength, and which is to be explained only on the ground of that rapt communion with God which Raphael depicts. Correggio's "Ecce Homo" is a representation of the suffering Saviour. All these have something of their own to tell us about Jesus—they bear witness to the grace and gentleness, the blazing purity and holiness, the quiet strength and suffering of Him who they believed had bought them with a price.

It is impossible for us now to follow the further course of Christian art; but in the main it has been true to the great Renascence tradition. Velasquez, in his picture of the Crucifixion, gives us the merest glimpse of the Saviour's face, leaving us to read into it what unutterable

depths of sorrowing love we may. Rembrandt's picture
of Jesus blessing little children is in the true succession
of the larger conception which came with the Renascence.
In our own time, Burne-Jones and Holman Hunt have
given no unworthy expression to their sense of the significance of Jesus. The well-known "The Light of the
World," by the latter, is perhaps the most moving Christian appeal ever uttered. You have the whole Gospel in
the attitude and gesture of the knocking, waiting Christ.

Second Week, Third Day

Who hath believed our report? and to whom hath the
arm of the Lord been revealed? For he grew up before
him as a tender plant, and as a root out of a dry ground:
he hath no form nor comeliness; and when we see him,
there is no beauty that we should desire him. He was
despised, and rejected of men; a man of sorrows, and
acquainted with grief: and as one from whom men hide
their face he was despised, and we esteemed him not.
Surely he hath borne our griefs, and carried our sorrows: yet we did esteem him stricken, smitten of God,
and afflicted. But he was wounded for our transgressions, he was bruised for our iniquities: the chastise-
ment of our peace was upon him; and with his stripes
we are healed. All we like sheep have gone astray;
we have turned every one to his own way; and the Lord
hath laid on him the iniquity of us all.—Isaiah 53: 1-6.

And yet, "what painter ever yet produced a wholly
satisfactory face of Christ?"[1] When Leon Bonnat, the
modern French realist, took a dead body from the Morgue
and hung it up on a cross and then, having painted it,
called the result, "The Crucifixion," we do not wonder that
he failed to do a convincing work. At least some degree
of sympathetic imagination is a prerequisite of such a
task.
Dr. Peabody has pointed out that "with but few exceptions, the Christ of the Masters is the Man of Sorrows,

[1] J. C. Van Dyke, "The Meaning of Pictures," p. 28.

whom it pleased the Lord to bruise and who is stricken for the transgressions of His people"; and it is a fair question whether in all this there is not an element of misrepresentation or at least of exaggeration. The interpretation of Jesus as the "suffering servant," the despised and rejected of men, has, it is said, caused a wholly inordinate interest to be attached to the darker and more tragic aspects of His history. Renan, for instance, accounts for the influence of Jesus by saying that "he was entranced by the vision of the divine life and gave himself with delight to its expression"; while Zangwill speaks of Him as "not the tortured God but the joyous comrade . . . the lover of warm life and warm sunlight, and all that is simple and fresh and pure and beautiful." In that case, of course, we must admit that the joyous young Shepherd of the Catacombs is a more faithful representation of Jesus than the tragic grandeurs of the Renascence Christ.

But it may be doubted whether this contrast is real. Why may not both views be essentially true and indeed mutually fulfilling? The revolt from the stress on the "suffering servant" interpretation of Jesus is of course largely due to the feeling that the traditional view of the Christian life as an affair of austere self-renunciation is hostile to the appreciation of beauty and to the joy of life. In point of fact, this is not true. "When a man begins to appreciate scenery," wrote a missionary in Africa some time ago, "it shows that our efforts are beginning to take effect."[2] It is also worth recalling that the earliest known landscape, painted in 1432 on the altarpiece of the Cathedral of St. Bavon at Ghent, in the famous "Adoration of the Mystical Lamb" by the brothers van Eyck already referred to, belongs to this period when men's eyes were chiefly turned to the Man of Sorrows. May we not infer from this that with a recovered sense of the redeeming grace of Jesus there came a new feeling

---

[2] "The East and the West," vol. IV, p. 82.

for the beauty of the world in which He had delighted?
Perhaps this is the real commentary on that deep word
—"By his stripes we are healed." "Medieval Art," says
Sir Wyke Bayliss, "in its first splendour was art trans-
figured by contact with the divine character and person
of Christ." It was not until the sixth century that Christian art ventured on an attempt to paint the Crucifixion;
but that was in the gloomy millennium and it came to
nothing. With the Renascence came a fuller and deeper
appreciation of the significance of the Son of Man, who
came to give His life a ransom for many and by that act
to give men "life more abundant"; and out of that new
abundance of life came first a revitalized art and then a
revitalized religion. The great discovery of that period
was assuredly this—that suffering is the price of redemption, that "without the shedding of blood there is no
remission of sins," nor anything else worth while. The
Man of Sorrows turned out to be the author of true joy.

"The one central figure that in the splendour of His
divine beauty consecrated Art for ever was that of Jesus."[3]

Second Week, Fourth Day

**And it came to pass, as he sat at meat in the house,
behold, many publicans and sinners came and sat down
with Jesus and his disciples. And when the Pharisees
saw it, they said unto his disciples, Why eateth your
Master with the publicans and sinners? But when he
heard it, he said, They that are whole have no need of a
physician, but they that are sick. But go ye and learn
what this meaneth, I desire mercy, and not sacrifice:
for I came not to call the righteous, but sinners.—Matt.
9: 10-13.**

We have seen how Art has in the main fastened on and
perpetuated two elements in the personality of Jesus, the
joyous simplicity of His bearing and the tragic grandeur
of His passion. This is not unnatural; for Art tends to

---

[3] "Christ and the Christian Character," p. 46.

seek its chief sustenance in the contemplation of the beauty and the tragedy of life.

This serves to illustrate a point which we shall encounter several times in the course of our study—namely, the almost inevitable way in which forward-looking men have found a "kindred spirit" in Jesus.

Another and the best example of this tendency is to be found in the fact that the Carpenter of Nazareth has been as rich a source of inspiration and courage as the Good Shepherd or the Suffering Saviour. There has hardly been a great "rebel" from John Ball to John Brown who has not sought and found his justification in Jesus; and every man who has had a feeling for the "common people," the great human mass in all its need and its possibilities, has found strength and courage in the story and example of Jesus.

Dr. Peabody has put on record a number of statements made by German working men about Jesus.[4] "Christ was a true friend of the working people," said one of them (and we need not quote any other), "not in His words alone but in His deeds." And when Dr. Abbott longed that the working men of England should say: "We used to think that Christ was a fiction of the priests . . . but now we find that He was a man, after all, like us, a poor working man who had a heart for the poor . . . now we understand this, we say, though we do not understand it all or anything like it, He is the man for us," he was only anticipating a day when a meeting of workers in Hyde Park in London gave "three cheers for Jesus Christ."

The sense of this broad fundamental human appeal of Jesus is, of course, no new thing. When Wyclif's "poor priests" were impregnating the peasantry of England with those social ideals which led up to the Peasants' Revolt, when John Ball the "mad priest of Kent" led the men of Kent to fight the social oppression of the time, William

---

[4] In "Jesus Christ and the Social Problem."

Langland gave expression in verse to the spirit which inspired this insurgency:

"For our joy and our health, Jesus Christ of heaven
In poor man's apparel pursueth us ever; . . .
For all we are Christ's creatures, and of His coffers rich
And brethren of one blood, as well beggars as earls."

Langland's great poem "Piers Plowman" is the poor man's Odyssey. Piers Plowman, the "hero" of the poem, is indeed no other than Jesus Himself—"the people's man, the people's Christ, poor humanity adorned with love, hardworking humanity armed with indignation, sympathetic humanity clad in the intelligence that knows all —and makes allowances; at one time setting highborn ladies to work, at another attacking the insolent priest, at another calling upon Famine to help him against the loafing growling wastrel of the streets; but always encouraging the penitent sinful, helping the weak, leading the way in the great journey, a strange figure, Christ in humanity, humanity Christ-clothed, neither all a poor man, nor all a ploughman, nor all a Jesus, but fading and vanishing and reappearing in all forms of His humanized divinity and ending as the Christ-conqueror that from the Cross went down and burst the doors and defied the brazen guns of hell."[5]

Second Week, Fifth Day

Since then the children are sharers in flesh and blood, he also himself in like manner partook of the same; that through death he might bring to nought him that had the power of death, that is, the devil; and might deliver all them who through fear of death were all their lifetime subject to bondage. For verily not of angels doth he take hold, but he taketh hold of the seed of Abraham. Wherefore it behoved him in all things to be made like unto his brethren, that he might be a merciful and faithful high priest in things pertaining to God, to make

---

[5] Arthur Burrell, Introduction to "Piers Plowman," p. x, (Everyman's Library).

propitiation for the sins of the people. For in that he himself hath suffered being tempted, he is able to succour them that are tempted.—Heb. 2: 14-18.

The identification of Jesus with humanity which we have seen in "Piers Plowman" is not confined to William Langland. When we come to study Mazzini in detail, we shall find him full of the same thought. Nor is it in the least a forced or arbitrary interpretation, for it is in a very real sense what Jesus Himself meant when He called Himself the "Son of Man," the typical, representative, ordinary man—not merely one of us, but all of us. And it may be questioned whether if an instinctive human response to an idea is a guarantee of its truth, any idea is more completely validated than this. Is there any one who can fail to feel the essential truth of the vision recorded by the great Russian Turgeniev?

"I saw myself, a youth, almost a boy, in a lowpitched wooden church. The slim wax-candles gleamed, spots of red, before the old pictures of the Saints. There stood before me many people, all fair-haired peasant heads. From time to time, they began swaying, falling, rising again, like the ripe ears of wheat when the wind in summer passes over them. All at once a man came up from behind and stood beside me. I did not turn towards him, but I felt that the man was Christ. Emotion, curiosity, awe overmastered me. I made an effort and looked at my neighbour. A face like everyone's, a face like all men's faces. The eyes looked a little upward, quietly and intently; the lips closed, not compressed; the upper lip as it were resting on the other; a small beard parted in two; the hands folded and still; and the clothes on him like everyone's. 'What sort of Christ is this?' I thought. 'Such an ordinary, ordinary man. It cannot be.' I turned away, but I had hardly turned my eyes from this ordinary man when I felt again that it was really none other than Christ standing beside me. Suddenly my heart sank and I came to myself. Only then I realized that just such a face is the face of Christ—a face like all men's faces."

The moral involved in this thought has been beautifully put in a poem by Alice Meynell. Despite its Catholic and sacramentarian background, the truth is no less valid for Protestants:

> "O Christ, in this man's life
> This stranger who is thine—in all his strife
> All his felicity, his good and ill
> In the assaulted stronghold of his will;
>
> I do confess Thee here,
> Alive within this life; I know Thee near
> Within this lonely conscience, closed away
> Within this brother's solitary day.
>
> Christ in his unknown heart,
> His intellect unknown, this love, this art,
> This battle and this peace, this destiny
> That I shall never know, look upon me.
>
> Christ in his numbered breath,
> Christ in his beating heart and in his death,
> Christ in his mystery! From that secret place,
> And from that separate dwelling, give me grace!"

It surely must be true that we shall not see the face of Jesus Christ except as we discern it in each other's faces; or, to put it in another way, without a vivid social sense we shall not descry all the meaning of "that one Face."

Second Week, Sixth Day

And from thence he arose, and went away into the borders of Tyre and Sidon. And he entered into a house, and would have no man know it: and he could not be hid. —Mark 7: 24.

There are few writers of any great account in the Christian era in whose works we fail to find material for

some kind of estimate of Jesus. Oddly enough one of
these exceptions is Shakespeare.

It is a moot question whether Shakespeare was a
Catholic or a Protestant—a case can be made out for
either view; but anyhow his silence upon this subject
requires some explanation. Dean Stubbs inclines to think
that it was because the official theology of Puritan England appears "to be based on a Christianity from which
the personality of Christ Himself seems to have quite dis-
appeared."[6] This judgment upon early English Protestantism is, of course, open to serious question; but in
any case the explanation seems hardly adequate. The
bitterness of theological controversy certainly does not
make for clear views about Jesus; and it is not improbable
that the austere character of the young Puritanism of the
time repelled the playwright. Yet this does not seem to
be the whole explanation of Shakespeare's silence. It has
been suggested that it was, at least in part, due to the fact
that play-acting was in those days in such hands that
a reverent spirit might shrink from introducing the name
of Jesus on to the stage. If that were so, the poet's silence
speaks very plainly. But at least we do know that it was
neither ignorance nor neglect that caused his silence.
When he makes Portia say:

"Earthly power doth then show likest God's
When mercy seasons justice"

he is expressing what we recognize to be the central
principle of the Christian doctrine of the Atonement. But
stronger than the evidence of isolated passages is the
uniform witness of the poet to the true spirit of the
Christian morality. In his insistence upon "the divinity
of forgiveness, of perpetual mercy, of constant patience,
of everlasting gentleness, the stainless purity of thought
and motive, the clear-sighted perception of a soul of good-

------

[6] "The Christ of English Poetry," p. 131.

ness in things evil, the unfailing sense of the equal providence of justice, the royalty of witness to sovereign
truth,"[7] Shakespeare shows himself a Christian; and his
witness to Jesus, though more indirect, is no less powerful
than that of others whose estimate is stated with more
explicitness.

There appears to be a certain ubiquity about the figure
of Jesus; wheresoever we turn, we encounter Him or
see His footsteps. There is hardly any literary figure in
whose work He does not soon or late appear. Not indeed
that He is always welcome; but He is palpably a figure
to be reckoned with. No literature which professes to
be true to life can ignore Him; some account has to be
taken of Him. He cannot be hid. His challenge seems
inevasible. There was a man of great ability, prominent
in English literary life some years ago, who had society
at his feet, commanded a large following, and might have
established a tradition in literature had not a nameless
sin destroyed him. He was sent to prison for his crime;
and in prison he had time to think. Presently he came to
think about Jesus, and one of the most tragical things in
literature is this man's attempt to appraise Jesus. Yet
such as it was, it had to be done. "If I make my bed in
hell, Thou art there."

Second Week, Seventh Day

When therefore it was evening, on that day, the first
day of the week, and when the doors were shut where the
disciples were, for fear of the Jews, Jesus came and
stood in the midst, and saith unto them, Peace be unto
you. And when he had said this, he shewed unto them
his hands and his side. The disciples therefore were
glad, when they saw the Lord. Jesus therefore said to
them again, Peace be unto you: as the Father hath sent
me, even so send I you.—John 20: 19-21.

Naturally, as we have seen, individual judgments of

---

7 "The Christ of English Poetry," p. 126.

Jesus are influenced, both in content and in statement, by the personal factor; and there is consequently an endless variety in the word-vignettes and pen-portraits of Jesus which we find scattered throughout literature. Dostoievsky, whose mind was colored by a Russian nationalism expressing itself in the ideal of "a Christian peasant people," and who looked to Russia in time to reveal its own "Russian Christ" to the world, finds in Jesus a figure of incomparable and ultimate perfection. "I believe there is nothing lovelier, deeper, more sympathetic and more perfect than the Saviour; I say to myself with jealous love that not only is there no one else like Him, but that there could be no one. I would say even more. If any one could prove to me that Christ is outside the truth, and if the truth really did exclude Christ, I should prefer to stay with Christ and not with truth." "There is," he says elsewhere, "in the world only one figure of absolute beauty: Christ. That infinitely lovely figure is as a matter of course an infinite marvel." This is plainly a judgment informed by large mystical elements. Mr. Bernard Shaw, who brings a cold realism to his study of Jesus, sees a different picture. After Peter's confession at Cæsarea Philippi, Mr. Shaw sees Jesus consumed by what appears to him to be a foolish passion for martyrdom; yet he says: "I am no more a Christian than Pilate was, or you, gentle reader; and yet, like Pilate, I greatly prefer Jesus to Annas and Caiaphas; and I am ready to admit that, after contemplating the world and human nature for nearly sixty years, I see no way out of the world's misery but the way which would have been found by Christ's will if he had undertaken the work of a modern practical statesman." Mr. Shaw denies with a measure of justice that the characteristic Christian doctrines were peculiar to Christ, but, he adds, "for some reason the imagination of white mankind has picked out Jesus of Nazareth as *the* Christ, and attributed all the Christian doctrines to him." *For some reason,* observe, which Mr. Shaw does not

specify. It might be worth Mr. Shaw's while—and ours
—to try to discover that reason.

A company of English literary men, including Charles
Lamb, Hazlitt, Leigh Hunt, and others, one day fell to
discussing persons they would like to have met, and after
naming every possible name in the gallery of fame,
whether worthy or unworthy, Charles Lamb said in his
stuttering way to the company: "There is only one person
I can ever think of after this. . . . If Shakespeare was to
come into this room, we should all rise up to meet him;
but if that Person was to come into it we should all fall
and try to kiss the hem of His garment." *Why* should
they? That is the question which somehow or another
must be answered. Even "when the door was shut, Jesus
came and stood in the midst"; and we have to do something about it. To help us we have this great variety of
impressions and judgments concerning Him; and in the
detailed study of some of these we have more to learn.

SUGGESTIONS FOR THOUGHT AND DISCUSSION

"When the Son of Man shall come in His glory, it may
turn out that His Glory consists in a suit of workingman's
overalls." Discuss this statement.

It might be of interest if small copies of the pictures
referred to in the reading for this week could be secured
and studied. Some of them at least are sure to be pro-
curable at a good art dealer's store.

Consider some of the passages in the gospels in which
Jesus is spoken of as the "Son of Man" and test the
accuracy of the interpretation of the phrase given in the
fifth day's reading.

What do you think is the real point of the "kid" in the
Catacomb pictures?

CHAPTER III

The Poet of the Awakening—
Dante
(1265—1321)

Most people would agree that the world's three greatest
poets are Homer, Dante, and Shakespeare. But Dante
differs from his two great peers in that he might also be
included in the category of the world's greatest prophets.
Both Homer and Shakespeare have a message to men;
but they deliver it only indirectly, without meaning or
appearing to do so. But Dante has a gospel to preach
and he never forgets it. It is the proof of the unique
quality of his poetic genius that not all his preaching
interferes with the purely poetic greatness of his work.

To say that "The Divine Comedy" was written with a
moral purpose is, however, to make a broad statement
which covers a complex of elements, each of which has
to be disentangled from the central mass and properly
appreciated before the huge and many-sided significance
of the poem can be apprehended. For one thing, Dante
had vowed that he would, when he could discourse
worthily concerning Beatrice—which skill he says he
labored all he could to attain—write "concerning her
what hath not before been written of any woman." This
vow he discharged in "The Divine Comedy." It is
Beatrice who befriends and guides him in his strange
journey through Paradise, and, though in his scheme she
is the personification of divine philosophy, she never
ceases to be that Beatrice Portinari of Florence in whom

the flaming love of the poet discovered everything that was lovely and pure and of good report. So it comes to pass that "The Divine Comedy" is the most pure and exalted memorial of a human love in all literature.

But the poem is not only a love song; it is also a political tract, like some Old Testament prophecies. Italy, as Dante saw it, was in a state of unspeakable confusion. The Guelphs and Ghibellines were at each other's throats; and the issue between the factions was complicated by an incredible mass of treason and corruption, feud and hate. Not only was this internal trouble devastating the country, but Dante saw with great misgiving how French princes were watching their opportunity to serve their own ends at the expense of Italy. The Church, moreover, was corrupt; it had allowed its spiritual office to be obscured and enfeebled by papal lust of temporal power. The Popes were "laying waste the vineyard for which Peter and Paul died." They were using their spiritual prerogatives for material ends. But Dante, by the love he bore Italy and the Church, rose above this welter of intrigue and corruption, and, though himself a Guelph, understood that there was no hope for Italy except in "a firm hand which would repress the turbulent factions which rent her bosom." Out of this grew the poet's hope of a political Messiah—a hope which survived many a bitter disappointment. And Dante did not cease to preach in season and out of season the gospel of a spiritual church unfettered by temporal entanglements and of a united Italy freed from feud within and interference from without. Of this political gospel "The Divine Comedy" was the supreme expression.

It would be interesting to follow out in more detail these and other elements which go to make up the extraordinary historical and human interest of the poem; but our present purpose confines us to what may seem a narrower inquiry, though in point of fact our quest will lead us to what is the central and controlling thought of the whole book.

[The quotations in verse are from Cary's translation; those in prose from the translations in the Temple Classics. For anyone who desires to study "The Divine Comedy," a useful introduction may be found in P. H. Wicksteed's "Dante."]

DAILY READINGS

Third Week, First Day

John to the seven churches which are in Asia: Grace to you and peace, from him which is and which was and which is to come; and from the seven Spirits which are before his throne; and from Jesus Christ, who is the faithful witness, the firstborn of the dead, and the ruler of the kings of the earth. Unto him that loveth us, and loosed us from our sins by his blood; and he made us to be a kingdom, to be priests unto his God and Father; to him be the glory and the dominion for ever and ever. Amen. Behold, he cometh with the clouds; and every eye shall see him, and they which pierced him; and all the tribes of the earth shall mourn over him. Even so, Amen.

I am the Alpha and the Omega, saith the Lord God, which is and which was and which is to come, the Almighty.

I John, your brother and partaker with you in the tribulation and kingdom and patience which are in Jesus, was in the isle that is called Patmos, for the word of God and the testimony of Jesus. I was in the Spirit on the Lord's day, and I heard behind me a great voice, as of a trumpet saying, What thou seest, write in a book, and send it to the seven churches.—Rev. 1: 4-11.

Dante was born in Florence in 1265; and he is by far the greatest figure we see in the ruddy dawn of the human mind's awakening after the torpor of the sterile millennium. His education seems to have endowed him with a clearness and breadth of vision beyond his contemporaries. Walter Bagehot says of Milton that he had "an ascetic nature in a sheath of beauty"; and this is equally true of Dante. Austerity and a keen warm sense of beauty were wedded in his nature with a perfect congruity. His pure love for Beatrice made his moral sense a burning passion, and his strong religious feeling made him such a prophet as the world had not seen since John the Baptist and Paul the Apostle. In that wilderness of feud and faction and intrigue, he lifted his voice not uncertainly and without ceasing, plunging into the political vortex in which he saw Florence and Italy involved, in the hope that he might bring something of order out of the confusion. But the enemy prevailed, and in 1300 Dante was banished from his own fair city of Florence. In the nineteen years that followed, he composed "The Divine Comedy."

Three great Christian scriptures were composed during enforced seclusion; and they are all records of visions. From lonely Patmos came the Apocalypse; from Bedford Jail came "The Pilgrim's Progress"; and Dante produced "The Divine Comedy" in exile.

The poem is in three parts—the visions of Hell, Purgatory, and Paradise. Through Hell and Purgatory the poet is guided by Virgil, the personification of human philosophy, while Beatrice, the personification of divine philosophy, leads him through the ascending cycles of Paradise. The poem is an account of what the poet saw on this strange journey. Interpolated here and there are philosophical and theological discussions, which are inserted with so much skill that they rarely seem incongruous. Contemporary allusions, which might conceivably have seemed inapposite in an imaginative work of this character, nevertheless take their place quite easily. So complete was Dante's vision of past, present, and future, so deeply was he sensible of the intimate relations of the material and spiritual worlds, so vast and so exceedingly exact was his survey of the sweep of the moral order, so profound his insight into human history and his reading of human life, that he was able to weld into one organic whole all the facts of his knowledge and experience, the conclusions of his philosophy and his theology. So true was his sense of the fitness of things, so keen was his penetration through the form to the abiding reality, that his poem has never lost its bloom and the freshness of its youth. It still remains, in spite of much that was purely local and temporary in its reference, a human document of universal and inexhaustible significance.

Third Week, Second Day

And they send unto him certain of the Pharisees and of the Herodians, that they might catch him in talk. And when they were come, they say unto him, Master, we know that thou art true, and carest not for any one: for thou regardest not the person of men, but of a truth teachest the way of God: Is it lawful to give tribute unto Cæsar, or not? Shall we give, or shall we not give? But he, knowing their hypocrisy, said unto them, Why tempt ye me? bring me a penny, that I may see it. And they brought it. And he saith unto them, Whose is this image and superscription? And they said unto him, Cæsar's. And Jesus said unto them, Render unto Cæsar the things that are Cæsar's, and unto God the things that are God's. And they marvelled greatly at him.—Mark 12: 13-17.

We shall not understand Dante's way of looking at things unless we remember at what point of time he appeared. He is, as has already been said, the outstanding figure in a period of transition, a period heralding another, the importance of which is second only to the coming of Jesus. It may rightly be regarded, in the words of one of his commentators, as "the great morning star of modern enlightenment." But Dante, like all other persons who have stood in similar places, was in a very real sense a product of the past as well as a herald of the future. During that dreary period which had lasted for nearly a thousand years before Dante's time, there had been flowing a stream of true piety. This piety naturally took its color from the prevailing Catholic idea, the growth of which is the chief external fact of church

history during that period. It had, however, no affinity
with the passion then prevalent at Rome to acquire
authority of a temporal character. When Rome had been
sacked by the Huns and Goths, what was of value in its
spirit and its institutions was preserved by the Church.
Unfortunately for the Church, it had been seized with
the craving for temporal power, and this craving suffered
no abatement with the passing of time. But there were
those who looked suspiciously upon this development and
regarded it as an evil and alien thing, and it was to this
succession that Dante belonged. The empire of the
Church was in his view wholly and exclusively spiritual;
and when it entered the political field, it was going out of
its own province. To use its power to gain secular
authority was to prostitute it, to render to Cæsar what
was God's. Cæsar had his own place and his own business; but that was not in the Church.

Rome, said Dante,

> "Was wont to boast two suns, whose several beams
> Cast light on either way, the world's and God's.
> One since hath quenched the other; and the sword
> Is grafted on the crook; and so conjoined
> Each must perforce decline to worse."

Dante held to the doctrine of the "two societies"; and
it is this doctrine which is reflected in the passage just
quoted. This doctrine was that there were in the world
two societies—the temporal, of which the Emperor was
head, and the spiritual, of which the Pope was head, each
independent and sovereign within its own sphere. It appeared to Dante that it was "as monstrous for the Pope
to seek political influence and to use his spiritual forces
for political ends as he would have judged it for the
Emperor to exercise political tyranny over the faith of
Christians."[1]

---

[1] Wicksteed, "Dante," p. 17.

Third Week, Third Day

I therefore, the prisoner in the Lord, beseech you to walk worthily of the calling wherewith ye were called, with all lowliness and meekness, with longsuffering, forbearing one another in love; giving diligence to keep the unity of the Spirit in the bond of peace. There is one body, and one Spirit, even as also ye were called in one hope of your calling; one Lord, one faith, one baptism, one God and Father of all, who is over all, and through all, and in all. But unto each one of us was the grace given according to the measure of the gift of Christ. Wherefore he saith,

When he ascended on high, he led captivity captive,
And gave gifts unto men.

(Now this, He ascended, what is it but that he also descended into the lower parts of the earth? He that descended is the same also that ascended far above all the heavens, that he might fill all things.) And he gave some to be apostles; and some, prophets; and some, evangelists; and some, pastors and teachers; for the perfecting of the saints, unto the work of ministering, unto the building up of the body of Christ.—Eph. 4: 1-12.

What is the Catholic idea? Froude has put it in this way: "At last He (that is, Jesus) passed away to heaven; but while in heaven, He was still on the earth. His body became the body of His church, not in metaphor but in fact—this very material body in which and by which the faithful would be saved. His flesh and blood were thenceforward to be their food. . . . As they fed on it, it would grow into them and it would become their real body." This confusion of natural and spiritual is bewildering to a Protestant mind; but if Catholicism has insisted overmuch upon the connection of spirit and matter, it is probable that Protestantism has underestimated its importance. Certainly the doctrine of the Church as the material body of Christ is foreign and unintelligible to the Protestant; and the doctrine of transubstantiation requires an act of faith of which a person of Protestant background is rarely capable. Yet when we have made the necessary allowance for the excess of emphasis upon the material form, there is a truth in the Catholic idea which Protestants cannot afford to neglect.

St. Paul uses the word *ecclesia* in two different but related senses. He applies it first of all to separate communities of believers; the second use is wider. It does not refer to the Church as the aggregate of the local communities, or an ideal society not yet realized on the earth. It is neither so concrete as the one nor so abstract as the other. What the word in this large sense is intended to cover, it is difficult to define precisely. It was something which existed in and subsumed each separate community—the underlying life, of which the local society was a distinct and individual embodiment. And this underlying life was the historical continuation of the life of Jesus. This life entered into the Christian societies; and as once Christ had become incarnate in a body of flesh, so He was incarnated afresh in a body of believers. The Church is His body. But there is no warrant for identifying this body with a particular society. That is the Roman error. The body of Christ is the body of all true believers; and that is the true Catholic idea.

But the Church was to Dante something more than a society or a corporation of which he could give a theological account. It was a "lovely flower,"

> "The fair bride who with the lance and nails
>   Was won."

His heart went out to it with a passionate intensity. In it were involved the hopes of a race; through it the great increasing purpose was destined to be accomplished. When he saw it prostituted to meaner ends, his soul was aflame with indignation. At a time when the superficiality and the trifling of its ministers were obscuring its supreme offices, he cried:

44

"Christ said not to his first conventicle,
'Go forth and preach impostures to the world,'
But gave them truth to build on, and the sound
Was mighty on their lips; nor needed they
Beside the Gospel other spear or shield
To aid them in their warfare for the faith."

The business of the Church was to kindle faith by proclaiming the Gospel. The sacraments do not take the first place in Dante's view, as they do in traditional Catholicism.

Third Week, Fourth Day

For not unto angels did he subject the world to come, whereof we speak. But one hath somewhere testified, saying,

What is man, that thou art mindful of him?
Or the son of man, that thou visitest him?
Thou madest him a little lower than the angels;
Thou crownedst him with glory and honour,
And didst set him over the works of thy hands:
Thou didst put all things in subjection under his feet.

For in that he subjected all things unto him, he left nothing that is not subject to him. But now we see not yet all things subjected to him. But we behold him who hath been made a little lower than the angels, even Jesus, because of the suffering of death crowned with glory and honour, that by the grace of God he should taste death for every man. For it became him, for whom are all things, and through whom are all things, in bringing many sons unto glory, to make the author of their salvation perfect through sufferings. For both he that sanctifieth and they that are sanctified are all of one: for which cause he is not ashamed to call them brethren, saying,

I will declare thy name unto my brethren,
In the midst of the congregation will I sing thy praise.

And again, I will put my trust in him. And again, Behold, I and the children which God hath given me.—Heb. 2: 5-13.

The promise of Jesus to be with His own to the end of the world was taken by medieval Catholicism to mean that He would be and was represented by the Church. The gift of Pentecost made the Church the representative and the agent, and its head the vicar, of Christ on earth. His personal presence as a direct influence in the Church and the world was prominent only in the minds of mystically disposed persons; it played little part in the official view. It was almost inevitable, therefore, that Dante should place his vision of Christ in the third part of his poem, his ascent through Paradise; and there he sees Him as the central glory of the army of the redeemed.

The ruling idea in Dante's conception of Christ is His character as redeemer. He thinks of Him as "Christ, son of the supreme God and son of the Virgin Mary, very man, who was slain by us to bring life, who was the light which enlightens us in darkness."[2] And the emphasis upon the redeeming quality of the death of Christ is a constant element in Dante's view of Jesus. It was to this end that He became incarnate—"the Son of God willed to load Himself with our pain." He fully accomplished His purpose. He appeared in Hell, preaching to the spirits in prison,

> "A puissant one,
> With victorious trophy crowned."

This victory was won on the "tree," whither

> "Christ was led
> To call on Eli, joyful, when He paid
> Our ransom from His vein."

The memory of our Lord's death remains on earth as the great motive of love to God, while in Paradise it has given Him a name which is above every name. Dante sees the hosts of Christ's triumph—

---

[2] This passage is not from "The Divine Comedy," but from a prose work called *"Convito"* (The Banquet) Chap. VI.

"In bright preeminence so saw I there
  O'er million lamps a sun, from whom all drew
  Their radiance, as from ours the starry train;
  And through the living light, so lustrous glowed
  The substance that my ken endured it not";

and in another place—

"In fashion as a snow-white rose lay then
  Before my view the saintly multitude
  Which in His own blood Christ espoused."

This is the setting in which Dante places Christ—far above all the principalities and powers and every name that is named; yet while this shows how wonderful Christ appeared to Dante, it carried with it a grave defect. It had the result of removing Christ out of real touch with the actual life of men.

Third Week, Fifth Day

Having then a great high priest, who hath passed through the heavens, Jesus the Son of God, let us hold fast our confession. For we have not a high priest that cannot be touched with the feeling of our infirmities; but one that hath been in all points tempted like as we are, yet without sin. Let us therefore draw near with boldness unto the throne of grace, that we may receive mercy, and may find grace to help us in time of need.—Heb. 4: 14-16.

"The white rose of the Divina Commedia" says Sir Wyke Bayliss, alluding to the last passage quoted, "is the great company of the redeemed, the petals are individual believers. And as a rose, even a white rose, deepens in colour towards the heart of it, so the wide circle of this saintly host as they approach the center becomes incarnadine with the very life-blood of Christ."

Of the glory of Christ in the midst of the redeemed, Dante confesses himself unable to give an adequate account; but he says that those who will themselves see that

glory will understand the reason. The quadrant in Mars
"so flashed forth Christ that I may not find example
worthy."

> "But whoso takes his cross and follows Christ
>   Will pardon me for that I leave untold
>   When in the fleckered dawning, he shall spy
>   The glitterance of Christ."

Observe that here the terms of seeing the glory of Christ
are the taking of the cross, and following Christ. This
is, of course, good evangelical teaching.

But Dante was so steeped in the notions of medieval
Catholicism that he does not think the vision possible
unless it be mediated through the Virgin Mary.

>   "Now raise thy view
> Unto the visage most resembling Christ,
> For in her splendour only shalt thou win
> The power to look on Him."

The place of Mary in the Catholic scheme owes its
origin probably to several circumstances. It represents
the survival of a pagan tradition, which was gathered up
into Christianity probably in Asia Minor. But this does
not mean that it does not correspond to a real human
need. The frequency with which the Madonna was
painted and the place she came to occupy in Catholic
devotion prove that some human craving was being met.
This was in part the absence from the current conception
of God of the quality usually attributed to motherhood;
and this is certainly an element in a complete view of
God. For fatherhood and motherhood are complementary
and are fulfilled in each other; and they must be found
together in the ultimate source of life. But probably the
greatest reason for the popular devotion to Mary lay in
the distance which had been placed between Christ and
the soul.

The tendency of the Church has been on the whole to

forget the humanity of Jesus and to emphasize His
divinity. Catholic dogma taught that He was very God
and true man; and Dante expresses this view consistently.
He sees the dual nature of Jesus in the reflection of the
griffin in the eyes of Beatrice.[3] Yet there was a feeling
that He dwelt in

> "Heavens too high for our aspiring,"

and the craving for the human touch has found expression
in more than one way. The doctrine of the "Sacred
Heart," that human heart of Christ which is in the midst
of heaven,

> "A heart that hath a mother and a treasure of red blood,
> A heart that man can pray to and feed upon for food,"

and that is even now

> "beating hot with love of me,"[4]

is an obvious device for recovering the point of contact
with the human element in Christ. The worship of Mary
belongs to the same cycle of longing. And these things
arise from the success with which the thought of the
Church has exalted Christ and so seemingly put Him
out of ordinary human reach. But we have not so learned
Christ.

Third Week, Sixth Day

**But . . . a righteousness of God hath been manifested,
being witnessed by the law and the prophets; even the
righteousness of God through faith in Jesus Christ unto
all them that believe; for there is no distinction; for
all have sinned, and fall short of the glory of God; being
justified freely by his grace through the redemption that
is in Christ Jesus: whom God set forth to be a propitiation, through faith, by his blood, to shew his righteousness, because of the passing over of the sins done afore-**

---

[3] The griffin was frequently used as a symbol of Christ, the eagle
head representing His divinity, and the lion body His humanity.
[4] F. W. Faber, *Hymns*, pp. 114, 115.

time, in the forbearance of God; for the shewing, I say, of his righteousness at this present season: that he might himself be just, and the justifier of him that hath faith in Jesus.—Rom. 3: 21-26.

The main concern of "The Divine Comedy" is with the vast and perplexing problem of sin. Christian theology has always regarded the fact of sin as the starting point of all doctrinal discussion; and Dante states the case in all its bearings as he sees it.

In the "Inferno" he shows the nature and consequences of sin. "The wages of sin is death" and this living death descends in cycle below cycle to ever more unspeakable depths of utter ruin.

The "Purgatorio" begins to proclaim a message of grace and hope. Repented and renounced sin is seen bearing the full measure of its consequences—no longer as a punishment, however, but as a discipline. The doctrine of the intermediate state is one upon which Scripture gives us no certain light; but the other element in the thought of Purgatory is, of course, one of the commonplaces of experience. The sins we commit against God may be forgiven, but the "deeds done in the body" follow us. Their significance is, however, changed by our repentance. In the "Inferno" they are a punishment; in the "Purgatorio" they constitute a process of chastening, by which the sinful disposition is eradicated and perfect holiness and fitness for Paradise attained.

Yet this, says our poet, is possible only on the ground of Christ's sacrifice. That which cleanses from all sin is the blood of our Lord Jesus Christ; and so when a soul is exalted into Paradise, it is another witness to the triumph of redeeming love. Dante sees Christ surrounded by a countless multitude of such souls, the petals of the white rose, each a seal of his victory. The unspeakable glory of the triumphant Redeemer is Dante's contribution to our thought of Christ. But the glory is the consequence of the humiliation. Paradise stands on Calvary.

It is a thought of some pertinence to us today whether we do not need to recover something of Dante's stark moral realism. Sir Oliver Lodge some time before the War told us that "the higher man of today" did not worry about his sins, but now after the War, when we have seen the awful certainty and scale of the retribution that follows a breach of the moral order, it is inconceivable that we shall not once more take the fact of sin more seriously than we have done in the past. If this is a moral universe, if its ground plan is a righteousness in which there is no variability or shadow of turning, then indeed obedience and disobedience become matters of life and death. It is doubtful whether any of our thinking is likely to be sound if we do not start from Dante's assumption that there is in the world, for men and nations, a single ultimate moral order, and that transgression of this order is inevitably followed by due recompense of reward. Certainly we shall miss much in our thought of Jesus if we fail to approach Him in this spirit of moral realism.

Third Week, Seventh Day

Then said Jesus unto his disciples, If any man would come after me, let him deny himself, and take up his cross, and follow me. For whosoever would save his life shall lose it: and whosoever shall lose his life for my sake shall find it. For what shall a man be profited, if he shall gain the whole world, and forfeit his life? or what shall a man give in exchange for his life?—Matt. 16: 24-26.

The foundation of the whole process by which a sinful man becomes a petal of the rose is—on the human side —*faith*. "To this realm," says Dante, "never rose one who believed not in Christ."

But faith in Dante's mind was something more than an act of emotional surrender. Evangelicalism has tended too much to make faith a matter of feeling. In a true faith, the whole man is engaged, in every part of him.

Faith, according to Dr. Du Bose, is "the entire disposition of our entire selves God-ward, holiness-ward." In any case, whatever else it may be, faith involves a definite moral decision; and it certainly contained that in Dante's view of it.

In the third canto of the "Inferno," our poet tells us how he is overwhelmed by dismal sounds as he enters the gate of Hell. These sounds, Virgil informs him, come from people whom neither Heaven nor Hell will receive.

"This miserable mode the dreary souls of those sustain, who lived without blame and without praise;

They are mixed with that caitiff choir of the angels who were not rebellious nor were faithful to God; but were for themselves;

Heaven chased them forth to keep its beauty from impair; and the deep Hell received them not, for the wicked would have some glory over them."

These luckless people, who "have no hope of death, whose blind life is so mean that they are envious of every other lot," are just those who sat on the fence and did not make the decisive moral surrender which gives point and meaning to life. They could not die, because they had never lived.

So we may fairly infer that faith in Dante's view is in the first instance not emotional, as the evangelical is apt to conceive of it, nor intellectual, as the official Catholic view appears to regard it, but an act of moral decision. It is the movement of the will toward the Will of God. Human faith in divine love—this is the pivot of the Gospel as Dante saw it; and this is the way by which men come to be planted in "the fair garden which flowereth beneath the rays of Christ."

The real message of Dante to us today is the need of recovering a plain and forthright ethical outlook upon the world and all that is in it, and an ethical approach to Jesus. Whether we, following Dante's road, shall see the precise vision he saw, is of course another question. We have a different inheritance; but we may be quite sure that the road does lead to a vision. To take up the Cross and to follow Christ is the passport into His presence.

SUGGESTIONS FOR THOUGHT AND DISCUSSION

"Where two or three are gathered together in my name, there am I in the midst of them." What light does this cast upon the nature of the Church? Compare it with the Catholic idea.

Collect the references in the New Testament to the Church as "the body of Christ" and "the bride of Christ," and discuss what each figure means.

Do you think that a recovery of the sense of sin is essential to a true understanding of Jesus?

How far do you suppose that Dante's division of the after-world into Hell, Purgatory, and Heaven is true? Is there any warrant for it in Scripture? How does it bear upon Omar Khayyam's saying, "I myself am heaven and hell"?

CHAPTER IV

The Poet as Reformer—Shelley
(1792—1822)

It is a far cry from Dante to Shelley. Nor is it only the distance of time which separates them: they differ profoundly from one another in their inherited background, in education, and in temperament. Moreover Dante, in spite of his independence of mind, was a devout believer; Shelley, on the other hand, professed to be an atheist.

It may seem a somewhat unpromising adventure to inquire of an atheist concerning Jesus. But two things may be said upon this point:

First, it is not merely interesting but important for our purpose to find out how Jesus would strike an atheist, a person who had deliberately thrown overboard all the beliefs in which he had been reared. This is, indeed, as near as we can get to such a picture of Jesus as would be impressed upon a virgin mind, and inasmuch as Shelley did not have "a grievance against Jesus," as some skeptical and unorthodox people are sometimes alleged to have, we ought to discover some material of value in his estimate of Jesus.

Second, it is really very questionable how far Shelley was what we nowadays would call an atheist. In his day any man who repudiated the orthodox tradition might have been called and might even call himself an atheist. To deny the commonly accepted idea of God is not necessarily to deny God. Indeed, the question may be fairly raised whether a poet can be an atheist at all. Certainly, he cannot be a pure rationalist or a pure materialist. It is the distinction of the poet that his very work is, so far as it goes, a *spiritual* interpretation of life; and this presupposes some kind and some measure of *faith,* that is, of belief in unseen reality. He may not give this unseen reality the name of God, but that does not matter so much as his assumption that there is an unseen reality.

Now, no one who is acquainted with Shelley's work can wholly accept his own description of himself as an atheist. He was, it is true, in open and vehement revolt against the orthodoxy of his time; he was frankly contemptuous of tradition. But it is quite plain to the careful student of Shelley that his mind was steadily moving onward to something like a real faith. He died when he was only thirty years of age; had he lived another thirty years, who knows whither his restless mind might not have led him? Inviting as such a speculation is, we must not here enter upon it. What we do know is that there is a discernible enlargement of view concerning man and life and the ultimate realities in Shelley's later thought, and that this development comes to an abrupt end. What might have been can never be written; but it may be worth while to record Browning's opinion: "I shall say what I think; had Shelley lived, he would finally have ranged himself with the Christians!"

DAILY READINGS

Fourth Week, First Day

Then saith Jesus unto them, All ye shall be offended in me this night: for it is written, I will smite the shepherd, and the sheep of the flock shall be scattered abroad. But after I am raised up, I will go before you into Galilee. But Peter answered and said unto him, If all shall be offended in thee, I will never be offended. Jesus said unto him, Verily I say unto thee, that this night, before the cock crow, thou shalt deny me thrice. Peter saith unto him, Even if I must die with thee, yet will

55

**I not deny thee. Likewise also said all the disciples.—
Matt. 26: 31-35.**

Shelley was peculiarly constituted. He had much more
than the average endowment of natural human insubordi-
nation. His chief characteristic appears to have been an
instinctive hatred of restraint; he was essentially a creature of impulse. "Shelley," says one of his critics, "was
probably the most remarkable instance of a purely impulsive character." The conduct of most men is governed
chiefly by impulse; but we recognize that impulse should
be subject to the discipline of reason and conscience.
Shelley's impulses, however, were but indifferently restrained; and when an impulse is aroused to movement
in such a personality, "it cramps the intellect, it pushes
aside the faculties, it constrains the nature, it bolts forward into action."

But in the case of most men of impulse, there is a
certain inevitable inconsistency which arises from the
number and variety of impulses which are latent in
human nature. On the other hand, the man of impulse
may be a man of one idea; and his impulses may all
emanate from a single universe of thought. The result
is that such a man will possess a character of some consistency and strength. Having a common origin in a
single supreme passion, his impulses will naturally have
also a common direction. This was the case with our
poet. The supreme passion of Shelley was for reforming
mankind; and it was from this spring that his impulses
habitually proceeded.[1]

It is clear that, admirable as such a character may be,
it lacks the balance necessary to accomplish results pro-
portionate to the energy which it expends. There is al-

---

[1] We are now concerned, of course, only with Shelley's nature as
it has affected his literary work. If we were engaged in a complete
analysis of Shelley, we should have to note such things as the morbid
sensitiveness which sent him on sudden and inexplicable travels, first
all over Great Britain and afterwards on the continent of Europe,
and accounts largely for his vagrant and stormy life.

ways a wide margin of distortion and exaggeration, both in word and in deed, which is sheer waste of power. One of the first conditions of substantial and effective service in reform is a patient study of all the relevant facts. From things as they are to things as they should be is a journey which no man can help the race to accomplish who does not quite frankly face the things that are just as they are. No strong language, no volume of emphatic statements, can make up for this elementary defect. It was at this point that Shelley failed. He had the type of mind that runs instinctively to generalizations. He had none of the patience which seeks out diligently the data necessary to reform or to sound judgment. This gave him something of the character of a firebrand; and firebrands are apt to give out more smoke than light. At the same time it must be remembered that Shelley's exaggerations and distortions are due to a quick sympathy with the suffering and the oppressed and a hot passion for liberty. "It was," says Professor Dowden, "the sufferings of the industrious poor that specially claimed his sympathy; and he thought of publishing for them a series of popular songs which should inspire them with heart and hope." These songs appeared after Shelley's death; and, like other of his songs, they were wrung out of him by his poignant sense of "man's inhumanity to man."

Fourth Week, Second Day

Whence then cometh wisdom?
And where is the place of understanding?
Seeing it is hid from the eyes of all living,
And kept close from the fowls of the air.
Destruction and Death say,
We have heard a rumour thereof with our ears.
God understandeth the way thereof,
And he knoweth the place thereof.
For he looketh to the ends of the earth,
And seeth under the whole heaven;
To make a weight for the wind;
Yea, he meteth out the waters by measure.

When he made a decree for the rain,
And a way for the lightning of the thunder:
Then did he see it, and declare it;
He established it, yea, and searched it out.
And unto man he said,
Behold, the fear of the Lord, that is wisdom;
And to depart from evil is understanding.
                                    —Job 28: 20-28.

A modern novelist has told the world that the writer of drama and romance finds his characters in himself. The persons who move across the stage are at bottom incarnations of some aspect of the writer's self, colored and shaped to some extent by his observation of other folk; and a play or a story written under these conditions becomes a mirror of the writer's own soul. Most firstclass fiction carries between the lines large elements of autobiography and self-revelation. But there is in all this a very real danger. The writer may present as a complete philosophy what is after all only a private view of life. He may suppose that his own soul is a full clue to the whole of experience; and consequently he may become contemptuous and impatient of views that are incongruous with his own.

This was peculiarly the case with Shelley. He thought that he read the heart of humanity in his own heart. "The characters which he delineates have all this kind of pure impulse. The reforming impulse is especially felt. In almost every one of his works there is some character of whom all we know is that he or she had a passionate disposition to reform mankind. We know nothing else about them and they are all the same."[2] Browning makes the same point concerning Shelley: "Not with the combination of humanity in action, but with the primal elements of humanity, he has to do; and he digs where he stands, preferring to seek them in his own soul as the

_____
[2] Walter Bagehot, "Literary Studies," Vol. I, p. 81.

nearest reflex of the absolute mind." Mankind was just Shelley writ large.

This quality of our poet has two consequences of importance. The first is that Shelley's whole view of life, and therefore the whole complexion of his work, was colored by the feeling that the great evil which poisoned life was the restraining influence of established institutions. These stood in the way of reforming impulse; and whether religious, political, or social, they all came under his lash. And over against them he raised the standard of what he called liberty. In his mind, liberty consisted in the removal of these cramping institutions; and the true man was he who, like himself, had revolted against them. This is the theme of the two great poems, "The Revolt of Islam" and "Prometheus Unbound." It is pertinent to observe that the established religion of his time was included by Shelley in his denunciations, and no man was free until he had broken with it.

Second, since he tended to regard himself as the mirror of humanity, he would naturally tend to seek himself in Jesus, to find in Jesus that which he chiefly felt himself to be. We shall find that this is the case. Indeed, it is more so with Shelley than with most men, because of his very pronounced and self-conscious individuality. Just as he read himself into other men and created his characters on his own image, so when he comes to contemplate Jesus, it is himself that he finds there, and he gives us a picture of Jesus which is a refined and sublimated version of himself.

Fourth Week, Third Day

To whom then will ye liken God? or what likeness will ye compare unto him? The graven image, a workman melted it, and the goldsmith spreadeth it over with gold, and casteth for it silver chains. He that is too impoverished for such an oblation chooseth a tree that will not rot; he seeketh unto him a cunning workman to set up a graven image, that shall not be moved. Have ye

not known? have ye not heard? hath it not been told you
from the beginning? have ye not understood from the
foundations of the earth? It is he that sitteth upon the
circle of the earth, and the inhabitants thereof are as
grasshoppers; that stretcheth out the heavens as a cur-
tain, and spreadeth them out as a tent to dwell in: that
bringeth princes to nothing; he maketh the judges of
the earth as vanity. Yea, they have not been planted;
yea, they have not been sown; yea, their stock hath not
taken root in the earth: moreover he bloweth upon them,
and they wither, and the whirlwind taketh them away as
stubble. To whom then will ye liken me, that I should
be equal to him? saith the Holy One. Lift up your eyes
on high, and see who hath created these, that bringeth
out their host by number: he calleth them all by name;
by the greatness of his might, and for that he is strong
in power, not one is lacking.—Isa. 40: 18-26.

We must first consider Shelley's revolt from religion
and just what it amounted to. His attitude to the conventional religion of his time is one of uncompromising
antagonism; and as soon as he became independent, he
embraced atheism. But though he professed to be an
atheist, as we have already seen, it is not safe to take the
description as entirely accurate. He began by believing
that there was nothing but matter; but his poet's soul
could find no resting-place in the desert of materialism;
and, characteristically, he swung to the extreme opposite
pole and began to question whether there was matter.
After all, might not everything be spirit? And might not
these things we see and touch and handle be just parts and
manifestations of some great unseen spiritual reality?
Shelley came to believe, as his great critic, Walter Bagehot, observes, that "passing phenomena were imperfect
types and resemblances, imperfect incarnations, so to
speak, of certain immovable, eternal, archetypal realities."
But these realities had a common basis in the ultimate
One. And

"The One remains, the many change and pass,
    Heaven's light for ever shines, Earth's shadows fly;

Life like a dome of many-coloured glass
Stains the white radiance of Eternity,
Until Death tramples it to fragments."

It seems but a step from this to a belief in God; and
to this *One* Shelley does indeed give the name of God.
But Shelley's God, though he speaks of him in terms a
Christian might accept, is very far from being the Christian God. For the *One* of whom Shelley sings is in no
sense personal; and consequently he cannot be regarded
as possessing moral qualities. In his famous letter to
Lord Ellenborough,[3] Shelley says: "Moral qualities are
such as only a human being can possess. To attribute
them to the spirit of the Universe, or to suppose it is
capable of altering them, is to degrade God into man,
and to annex to this incomprehensible being qualities in-
compatible with any possible definition of its nature."
But where God is conceived of as devoid of moral qualities, there cannot be any deep religious feeling, at least
in the sense in which these words are commonly understood; and if God is impersonal or unmoral, the question
of any relation of personal dependence upon Him or
communion with Him, which is the very essence of religion, cannot possibly arise.

Shelley's God is therefore just *x,* the unknown quantity,
who is there, but of whom we cannot gain any knowledge.
This at least was his intellectual judgment upon the
matter; but it is plain that this did not satisfy Shelley's
whole man.

Fourth Week, Fourth Day

As the hart panteth after the water brooks,
So panteth my soul after thee, O God.
My soul thirsteth for God, for the living God:
When shall I come and appear before God?

---

[3] This "Letter to Lord Ellenborough" was written on the occasion
of the punishment of a London publisher, by imprisonment and pillory,
for alleged blasphemy in 1812. Lord Ellenborough was the condemning
judge.

My tears have been my meat day and night,
While they continually say unto me, Where is thy God?
These things I remember, and pour out my soul within
    me,
How I went with the throng, and led them to the house
    of God,
With the voice of joy and praise, a multitude keeping
    holyday.
Why art thou cast down, O my soul?
And why art thou disquieted within me?
Hope thou in God: for I shall yet praise him
For the health of his countenance.—Psalm 42: 1-5.

Martensen, the Scandinavian theologian, speaking of
certain thinkers whose intellectual attitude was similar
to Shelley's, says: "We think we can discern in them a
yearning and a striving, of which they themselves are
unconscious, after an ethical personal God such as their
system denies. In their moments of greatest enthusiasm,
they have experienced a need of holding intercourse with
that highest Idea as though it were a personal being.
Even in Spinoza a certain bent towards personality is
discernible; for example, where he speaks of intellectual
love to God and styles it a part of that infinite love with
which God loves Himself. Schiller, Fichte, and Hegel
were, too, stirred by a religious, an ethical mysticism
which contained the germs of a personal relation to God."
What this means is that men, though their intellects
deny a personal God, yet in their hearts seek after Him.
This same tendency is to be seen in Shelley. In "Alastor,"
he addresses the

> "Mother of this unfathomable World"

and asks her to

> "Favour my solemn song; for I have loved
> Thee ever and Thee only. I have watched
> Thy shadow and the darkness of thy steps,
> And my heart ever gazes on the depth
> Of thy deep mysteries."

It is true that Shelley puts these words in Alastor's mouth; but if Alastor was not Shelley, then there never was a Shelley. This same craving manifests itself in a tendency to "personify isolated qualities or impulses—equality, liberty, revenge, and so on." This may be to some extent merely a poetic device; still it reflects the yearning of the soul for the over-soul. And the implications of this instinctive feeling have been stated by a modern scientist: "If the religious instincts of the human race point out to no reality as their object, then they are out of analogy with other instinctive endowments. Elsewhere in the animal world, we never meet with such a thing as an instinct pointing aimlessly."[4] That is to say, it is a fair assumption, on the analogy of nature, that the human craving for God means that there is a God to be craved for.

These then are the two elements in Shelley's mental background—his conception of the oneness of the ultimate reality and the real though unrecognized tendency to seek some kind of fellowship with the Unseen. Shelley might call himself an atheist; but it is plain at least that he had the substantial beginnings of a robust religious sense.

Fourth Week, Fifth Day

For the word of the cross is to them that are perishing foolishness; but unto us which are being saved it is the power of God. For it is written,

> I will destroy the wisdom of the wise,
> And the prudence of the prudent will I reject.

Where is the wise? where is the scribe? where is the disputer of this world? hath not God made foolish the wisdom of the world? For seeing that in the wisdom of God the world through its wisdom knew not God, it was God's good pleasure through the foolishness of the preaching to save them that believe. Seeing that Jews ask for signs, and Greeks seek after wisdom: but we

---

[4] Romanes, "Thoughts on Religion," p. 82.

preach Christ crucified, unto Jews a stumblingblock, and unto Gentiles foolishness; but unto them that are called, both Jews and Greeks, Christ the power of God, and the wisdom of God. Because the foolishness of God is wiser than men; and the weakness of God is stronger than men.—I Cor. 1: 18-25.

It will now be quite clear that in approaching Jesus, Shelley would exclude most of the conventional teaching about Him from his mind. The idea of incarnation was unthinkable to him, save only as the impersonal essence which stood for God in his mind is, as it were, incarnate in all things. That Jesus should be regarded as in any special or unique way the Incarnation of God, appeared to our poet a mere superstition, and the traditional view of redemption through the incarnate Son of God seemed the wildest foolishness. In "Queen Mab" (1813), one of his early poems, he assails the conception of the Atonement in a tone of bitter satire. After laying the responsibility for human sin at God's door, he goes on to describe the divine provision for dealing with sin.

> "One way remains,
> I will beget a Son, and he shall bear
> The sins of all the world. He shall arise
> In an unnoticed corner of the earth,
> And there shall die upon a cross, and purge
> The universal crime; so that the few
> On whom my grace descends, those who are marked
> As vessels to the honour of their God
> May credit this strange sacrifice and save
> Their souls alive; millions shall live and die
> Who ne'er shall call upon their Saviour's name,
> But unredeemed go to the gaping grave."

It is possible that we have become so habituated to the New Testament teaching of redemption that we have lost the sense of its staggering strangeness. Shelley stood remote from it and saw much of that uniqueness and unfamiliarity to which habit blinds us; but it was so com-

64

pletely foreign to his universe that in his impulsive way
he wrote it all off as an absurdity. This is one of those
cases where Shelley's disinclination to master the significance of all the facts of the case led him into a position
from which a little more patience would have saved him,
as indeed a maturer judgment ultimately did. "Queen
Mab" was the product of youthful and rather aggressive
atheism; and it is not difficult to believe that, in spite of
the great genius displayed by the poem, his wife was
right in saying that she thought his mature taste would
have condemned it. As a matter of fact, in 1821 he himself described it as "villainous trash."

To Shelley, then, Jesus would rank simply as a man;
and from what we know of Shelley's habit of mind, we
should be able to anticipate without much difficulty the
kind of character with which he would invest Him. Of
his admiration for Jesus there can be no question; but it
was inevitable that he should class Him among the goodly
company of reformers. "Jesus Christ was crucified," he
had written to Lord Ellenborough, before "Queen Mab"
had appeared, "because He attempted to supersede the
ritual of Moses with regulations more moral and humane;
his very judge made public acknowledgment of His innocence, but an ignorant and bigoted mob demanded the
deed of horror—Barabbas the traitor and murderer was
released. The meek reformer Jesus was immolated to the
sanguinary deity of the Jews." This passage shows a
characteristic misreading of the facts, but it shows clearly
the category in which Shelley placed Jesus. But the
ascription to Him of any character transcending that of
a reformer, Shelley put down as a superstition. It should,
however, be remembered that the role of reformer was
the highest and noblest in Shelley's scheme of things.

Fourth Week, Sixth Day

**Ye have heard that it was said, Thou shalt love thy
neighbour, and hate thine enemy: but I say unto you,**

**Love your enemies, and pray for them that persecute you;
that ye may be sons of your Father which is in heaven:
for he maketh his sun to rise on the evil and the good,
and sendeth rain on the just and the unjust. For if ye
love them that love you, what reward have ye? do not
even the publicans the same? And if ye salute your
brethren only, what do ye more than others? do not even
the Gentiles the same? Ye therefore shall be perfect,
as your heavenly Father is perfect.—Matt. 5: 43-48.**

In his "Essay on Christianity" (1816), Shelley makes
a serious attempt to estimate the significance of Jesus
and His teaching. At the outset, he acknowledges "his
extraordinary genius, the wide and rapid effect of his
unexampled doctrines, his invincible gentleness and be-
nignity, the devoted love borne to him by his adherents."
"We discover," he says later in the essay, "that he is the
enemy of oppression and of falsehood; that he is an advo-
cate of equal justice, that he is neither disposed to sanction
bloodshed nor deceit, under whatsoever pretences their
practice may be vindicated. We discover that he was a
man of meek and majestic demeanour, calm in danger, of
natural and simple thoughts and habits, beloved to adoration by his adherents, unmoved, solemn, severe." Shelley
had evidently read the gospels to some purpose; and the
picture he draws is open to no criticism. But one peculiar-
ity Shelley's portrait of Jesus has which is very luminous.
He finds it impossible to draw a picture to his own liking
without excising from the gospel narratives certain passages which appeared to be inconsistent with the character of Jesus—a proceeding neither scientific nor just. But
it shows that, to Shelley, Jesus seemed so altogether admirable that he would not allow the records of His life
(as he understood or misunderstood them) to cast an
inadvertent shadow upon His stainless beauty.

In his account of Jesus' teachings, Shelley makes a
brave attempt to reconcile it with his own view of things.
"God is represented by Jesus Christ as the power from
which and through which the streams of all that is delight-

ful and excellent flow, the power which molds as they pass all the elements of this mixed universe to the purest and most perfect shape which it belongs to their nature to assume. Jesus Christ attributes to this power the faculty of Will. How far such a doctrine in its ordinary sense may be philosophically true or how far Jesus Christ intentionally availed himself of a metaphor easily understood, it is foreign to the subject to consider. This much is certain, that Jesus Christ represents God as the fountain of all goodness, the eternal enemy of all evil, the uniform and unchanging motive of the salutary operations of the material world." This sounds very like Matthew Arnold's definition of God as "that stream of tendency, not ourselves, that makes for righteousness," but it is very remote from Jesus' own words: "After this manner, pray ye, *Our Father, who art in heaven,*" or "I know that Thou hearest me always." Though Shelley saw the beauty of Jesus, it is plain that he has not properly understood His mind.

Our poet, however, sees that Jesus' ethical teaching rests upon His conception of the moral nature of God; but it is quite in keeping with Shelley's habit of mind that he should find the distinctive element of the teaching to be the injunctions against revenge. "Jesus Christ instructed his disciples to be perfect as their Father in heaven is perfect, declaring at the same time his belief that this perfection requires the refraining from revenge and retribution in its various shapes." This is hardly a complete account of what Jesus meant by "perfection." That quality is no negative thing; it consists in love, a love that is, as Dr. Forsyth says, true to itself through everything, even to the loving of enemies. Of the way in which Jesus thought about human nature, Shelley gives an account which is just enough. "He simply exposes with the passionate rhetoric of enthusiastic love towards all human beings the misery and the mischiefs of that system which makes all things subservient to the subsistence of the

material frame of man. He warns them that no man can
serve two masters, God and mammon, that it is impossible
at once to be highminded and just and wise and to comply
with the accustomed forms of human society, seek power,
wealth, or empire, from idolatry of habit, or as the direct
instruments of sensual gratification." All of this, after
all, is only an extended way of saying an ancient word
which Jesus repeated at a memorable moment, and in
which He expressed the fundamental distinctiveness of
the nature of man—*"Man shall not live by bread alone."*

Fourth Week, Seventh Day

**And they come unto Bethsaida. And they bring to
him a blind man, and beseech him to touch him. And
he took hold of the blind man by the hand, and brought
him out of the village; and when he had spit on his eyes,
and laid his hands upon him, he asked him, Seest thou
aught? And he looked up, and said, I see men; for I behold them as trees, walking. Then again he laid his
hands upon his eyes; and he looked stedfastly, and was
restored, and saw all things clearly. And he sent him
away to his home, saying, Do not even enter into the
village.—Mark 8: 22-26.**

It is clear that Shelley has nothing particularly new
to tell us about Jesus. Indirectly, however, he has a good
deal to teach us. To begin with, we have in Shelley a
mind entirely emptied of all prepossessions in favor of
religion and altogether at enmity with all forms of orga-
nized religion; and it is plainly of some importance to
have seen how Jesus impresses such a mind. That there
was a certain change of intellectual position in the interval
between "Queen Mab" and the "Essay on Christianity"
is scarcely open to question. But this change is in no wise
comparable to the complete revolution of temper which
has taken place in the same interval. In the "Essay"
there is nothing of the bitter satire of "Queen Mab";
on the contrary, there is a sensible atmosphere of sympathy. The care alluded to already that nothing in the

gospel records themselves should sully the fame of Jesus, not even the supposed extravagances of the evangelists, shows how the figure of Jesus has influenced the poet's temper. Yet his vision yields him no adequate vision of Jesus. The disparity between the Christ of Shelley's "Essay" and the Jesus of the gospels is considerable. But is the story not told of one who, as sight came to him, saw men as trees walking? And the unclear vision of Shelley seems to be not so much the result of defective sight as the premonition of a growing and clearing sight. As he settled down to study Jesus, his eyes began to be opened. Who can tell, had not the angel of death come so early, but that Shelley might yet have seen vastly more in the face of Jesus? He had already traveled far from the days of "Queen Mab" by the time he came to write the "Essay." Whether he would have reached the traditional view of Jesus as we find it in the creeds, may be open to question; but he was beyond peradventure on the road to a larger and fuller vision.

We have seen how Shelley read his own passion for reform into Jesus, and in the same manner, he finds Jesus to be, like himself, a poet. Shelley, like all men of his temperament, believed intensely in himself and in his mission. That one should be a poet and a reformer was to attain the summit of manhood; and so Jesus appeared to Shelley. He was the "sublimest and most holy poet"; and also, "he tramples upon all received opinions, on all cherished luxuries and superstitions of mankind. He bids them cast aside the claims of custom and blind faith by which they have been encompassed from the very cradle of their being." Shelley tended overmuch to identify reform with mere iconoclasm; and in this passage, he was merely executing a portrait of himself. Yet does not all this illustrate the truth that the measure of our sympathy with a person is the measure of our understanding of him? This is true of Jesus, as of all other men. The kinship of poetic spirit and humane aspiration which Shelley found in Jesus became the measure of his understanding of Jesus. This, so far as it goes, is good and true; but it is not a sufficient ground for a complete judgment upon Jesus.

SUGGESTIONS FOR THOUGHT AND DISCUSSION

Look up in a good dictionary these terms: Atheist, Agnostic, Skeptic, Pantheist, Deist; and consider to what class Shelley belongs.

In what sense was Jesus a reformer? What did He reform? Sometimes He has been called a "revolutionary." Is this true? If so, in what sense?

What was Shelley thinking about when he said Jesus was a poet? Can you find any poetry in the gospels? Remember that you may have poetry without rhyme or meter.

Consider how much you can know of a man from— (a) *reading his life* and (b) *reading his books* or *studying his pictures*. What is it that you do not discover from these sources; and how or where can you discover this thing? Apply this to our knowledge of Jesus.

Consider the Seventh Day's Scripture reading as an interpretation of Shelley's spiritual life.

CHAPTER V

The Poet as Rebel—William Blake

(1757—1827)

William Blake is one of the strangest figures in the history of British art and literature. He ranks high both as artist and as poet; and he published his own poetry, illustrated by his own designs, printed from plates made by himself and by a process partly devised by himself. These productions are not merely curiosities of literature, but are also in their way masterpieces of art; and while they were sought for only by a small understanding circle of people in his own day, they have since been greatly coveted by lovers of beautiful things all the world over.

But before he was either artist or poet, Blake was a rebel. The student of Blake will find many points of similarity between him and Shelley, though it does not appear that they crossed each other's orbits. Blake was born long before Shelley and died some years after him; both alike reflect the unrest and the latent rebellion of their own age, which was the age of revolution. It is, indeed, only as we see them as characteristic figures of a turbulent period that we can properly appreciate them.

Blake, however, was much more of a rebel than Shelley. No man ever loved liberty with a deeper passion or hated any kind of bondage with a more perfect hatred than did William Blake. Wheresoever he saw men striking away their fetters, Blake did not hesitate to raise a cheer. During the days of the French Revolution, he went about

London wearing a red cap; and whether it was authority in religion, or convention in art, tradition in literature, or absolutism in politics, in so far as Blake believed it to hinder men's freedom, he assailed it with a vehemence that never relented. Naturally it was in the region of Art that his protest was loudest and his rebellion most unyielding; but he sang the praises of Wesley and Whitfield because they had dared to break through the dry formalism of the conventional religion of their own time; and he was one of that farseeing and courageous company of Englishmen who had the hardihood to side with the thirteen American colonies in their struggle for independence. He was the consistent devotee of liberty throughout his life.

But whereas Shelley was an intellectualist and a poet of ideas, Blake was a seer and a poet of visions. He professed to see visions in which he talked with the Old Testament prophets and some of the great personalities of history; and these visions were more real and immediate to him than the actualities of life. Whether we accept Blake's own view of these visions or not, it is beyond question that he was a seer of quite extraordinary power and originality. What seems to be true of him is that he lived consistently upon that shadowy border line which separates the waking world from the world of dreams. The fantastic results, both in his conversation and written work and, indeed, in his drawings, have tempted some to believe that Blake was mad. But two such formidable critics as Algernon Swinburne and G. K. Chesterton have finally dispelled the myth of Blake's insanity. Perhaps it is the case that Blake was, after all, wholly sane; and that we who live so exclusively in the world of sense are not altogether sane.

But the fact remains that Blake's writing and drawing are to a great extent obscure and difficult of interpretation. He invented a wild and staggering symbolism in order to convey his ideas; and since he left no clue to his symbolism, it is certain that large tracts of his writing will remain in impenetrable obscurity. Nevertheless, there is no ambiguity or obscurity about the main outlines of what he wished to say to the world. Blake lived in a time of revolution, and he had a gospel of reconstruction for that day which is not without its pertinence to ours.

It should not, however, be supposed that all Blake's poetry is obscure. On the contrary, some of his poems and lyrics are as clear and sparkling as a mountain stream. It is only in the so-called "prophecies" that he is hard and sometimes impossible to understand. Of these there are several—the chief and the noblest being "Jerusalem"—in which Blake has gathered up his whole philosophy of life.

[An excellent selection of Blake's works, both of the prophecies and the other poems, has recently been published by the Oxford University Press.]

DAILY READINGS

Fifth Week, First Day

For I know that in me, that is, in my flesh, dwelleth no good thing: for to will is present with me, but to do that which is good is not. For the good which I would I do not: but the evil which I would not, that I practise. But if what I would not, that I do, it is no more I that do it, but sin which dwelleth in me. I find then the law, that, to me who would do good, evil is present. For I delight in the law of God after the inward man: but I see a different law in my members, warring against the law of my mind, and bringing me into captivity under the law of sin which is in my members. O wretched man that I am! who shall deliver me out of the body of this death? I thank God through Jesus Christ our Lord. So then I myself with the mind serve the law of God; but with the flesh the law of sin.—Rom. 7: 18-25.

The starting point of Blake's thought is the sovereignty of the creative energy in man. The end of life is Art, creative imagination expressed in any medium, whether of substance or of sound, by which the human spirit may make itself articulate. Blake's God is the supreme artist; Jesus was the incarnation of the poetic or creative genius. "Prayer," inscribed Blake on one of his engravings, "is the study of Art. Praise is the practice of Art." "A Poet, a Painter, a Musician, an Architect—the man or woman who is not one of these is not a Christian." "The eternal body of man," he says in the same place, "is the imagination, that is, God himself, the divine body, Jesus. We are His members. It manifests itself in His works of Art; in eternity all is vision."

The point here is that God is the creator, but as God is immanent in all men, then men, too, are creative beings; and only as they are creative are they real men. The emphasis upon the divine indwelling is constant throughout Blake:

"Go tell them that worshipping God is honouring His gifts
  In other men; and loving the greatest men best; each according
To his power, which is the Holy Ghost in man; there is no other
God than that God, who is the intellectual fountain of humanity."

But Blake is well aware that this doctrine does not cover all the facts of life. Man does not live up to this view of him; and Blake has to take account of that fact which William James has called the "divided self." This fact Blake meets by enunciating a doctrine of conversion: "Man is born a spectre or Satan and is altogether an evil and requires a new self-hood continually, and must be changed into his direct contrary." This is a doctrine of original sin and conversion definite and clear enough to satisfy the most conservative Christian. But it does not follow that the new nature as Blake sees it will behave itself in the same manner as the converted person of the common tradition. According to the latter at its best, we are transformed into saints; according to Blake, if we are soundly converted, we are transformed into artists and poets. That is to say, conversion is the release of the divine urge of vision and creation which is latent in every man.

The trouble with man is twofold. First of all, he has trouble within himself. The poetic or creative energy through which manhood is to manifest itself is not the only ingredient of human nature. There are also in his composition the two powers of Desire and Reason. Man is right only when Desire and Reason balance each other and so enable the creative energy to express itself in an equable and unstrained fashion. But usually Desire and Reason are apt to be at cross-purposes and the result is inward chaos.

Desire, says our poet, is not to be suppressed; but equally is it not to be unbridled. He has a fine contempt for those who restrain Desire; they only succeed "because their desire is weak enough to be restrained." At the same time he sees that the undue exaltation of Desire is a peril. It leads to sensuality, "the vegetated life," as Blake calls it, to which all vision is denied. But Blake was more afraid of the supremacy of Reason than that of Desire. He calls Reason the

"Abstract objecting power that negatives everything;
 This is the spectre of man, the holy Reasoning Power
 And in its holiness is enclosed the Abomination of Deso-
    lation."

We shall have to inquire somewhat more particularly into Blake's hostility to Reason. Meantime we observe that it is his view that human perversity is due to the distortion of the poetic or creative energy in man by the excessive place occupied in his life either by Desire or by Reason. Whether Blake's psychology is sound or not is, of course, another story.

Fifth Week, Second Day

But when it was now the midst of the feast Jesus went up into the temple, and taught. The Jews therefore marvelled, saying, How knoweth this man letters, having never learned? Jesus therefore answered them, and said, My teaching is not mine, but his that sent me. If any man willeth to do his will, he shall know of the teaching, whether it be of God, or whether I speak from myself. He that speaketh from himself seeketh his own glory: but he that seeketh the glory of him that sent him, the same is true, and no unrighteousness is in him. Did not Moses give you the law, and yet none of you doeth the law? Why seek ye to kill me? The multitude answered, Thou hast a devil: who seeketh to kill thee? Jesus answered and said unto them, I did one work, and ye all marvel. For this cause hath Moses given you circumcision (not that it is of Moses, but of the fathers); and on the sabbath ye circumcise a man. If a man receiveth circumcision on the sabbath, that the law of Moses may not be broken; are ye wroth with me, because I made a man every whit whole on the sabbath? Judge not according to appearance, but judge righteous judgement.—John 7: 14-24.

It is said that "the goal of thought is one," and the task to which the human Reason sets itself is that of finding the "one," the underlying unity of things. It goes about this task first by studying things and grouping them according to their similarities. Then it tries to find a general statement, on the basis of the similarity, that is explanatory and true of each of these groups. Afterwards, it proceeds to compare and group these general statements, and to discover still longer generalizations which will cover and explain the first groups of general statements. It hopes some time to evolve one supreme general statement which will cover all the facts of life, and when it does that there will be no more need to think.

But it is not likely to do so. Life is, after all, a greater thing than thought; and thought is never able to keep pace with life. As a matter of fact, our generalizations

are being continually made out of date by the advances
of life and knowledge. For instance, when Dalton made
that great general statement which was known as the
atomic theory, it was supposed to be the last word about
the constitution of matter. Now we know that it is not.
Instead of speaking of molecules and atoms, we are speaking today of electrons and ions. At least we were doing
so a few years ago. Perhaps scientific thought has already moved beyond that.

Now the trouble here is that men come to regard these
general statements as absolute truths, and to harden them
into dogmas. When they become dogmas they resist the
further advance of thought; and presently it becomes a
sin to doubt their truth and a crime to resist them. In
the light of the best knowledge of the time it was once
believed that the sun revolved around the earth; to question the truth of this view was a sin; and for doing so
Galileo was imprisoned by the Inquisition. When Darwin
enunciated the evolution theory, he was assailed as an
atheist because he had dared to question the prevailing
theory of creation. And yet today we know that Darwin
was right. This does not mean, however, that Darwin
said the last word upon the subject; and it is possible
that the theory of evolution has already hardened into a
dogma which all men must accept. Nowadays we are
not likely to burn or to pillory men for disbelieving in
evolution; but perhaps a little later someone who has
gone beyond Darwin may be attacked as a corrupter of
youth. And so it goes on.

And Blake saw this kind of thing going on round
about him. He sees all around systems of dogma—in
philosophy, religion, politics, art, law, everywhere—which
imprison men's minds. He calls these systems "wheels,"
which bind and crush human personality; and the definitions and laws of the philosophers he calls "the limit
of opaqueness," a wall of darkness within which men's
minds are hopelessly caged. Bacon, Newton, Locke, and

all the formidable names of intellectual orthodoxy in his day, he assails with an untiring violence:

"For Bacon and Newton sheathed in dismal steel their
  terrors hang
 Like iron scourges over Albion; Reasonings like vast
  serpents
 Infold around my limbs, bruising my minute articulations.
 I turn my eyes to the schools and universities of Europe,
 And there behold the loom of Locke, whose woof rages
  dire
 Washed by the Water wheels of Newton; black the Cloth
 In heavy wreathes falls over every action; cruel works
 Of many wheels I view, wheel within wheel, with cogs
  tyrannic
 Moving by compulsion each other; not as those in Eden
  which
 Wheel within wheel in freedom revolve in harmony and
  peace."

Reason, which was meant to be the stabilizer of the human creative or poetic energy, had become its dark prison-house.

And it was not merely in philosophy that Blake saw this hard encaging dogmatism at work. It was destroying art; and in religion and morality it was tying men down to doctrines and laws which held the forces of life in thrall and forbade their flying free. Man was a slave in the bondage of reason-made systems; and Blake lived in order to shatter these bonds and to emancipate the slave.

Fifth Week, Third Day

And I saw a new heaven and a new earth: for the first heaven and the first earth are passed away; and the sea is no more. And I saw the holy city, new Jerusalem, coming down out of heaven from God, made ready as a bride adorned for her husband. And I heard a great voice out of the throne saying, Behold, the tabernacle of God is with men, and he shall dwell with them, and they shall be his peoples, and God himself shall be with them, and be their God: and he shall wipe away every tear from their eyes; and death shall be no more; neither shall there be mourning, nor crying, nor pain, any more: the first things are passed away. And he that sitteth on the throne said, Behold, I make all things new. And he saith, Write: for these words are faithful and true. And he said unto me, They are come to pass. I am the Alpha and the Omega, the beginning and the end. I will give unto him that is athirst of the fountain of the water of life freely. He that overcometh shall inherit these things; and I will be his God, and he shall be my son. But for the fearful, and unbelieving, and abominable, and murderers, and fornicators, and sorcerers, and idolaters, and all liars, their part shall be in the lake that burneth with fire and brimstone; which is the second death.—Rev. 21: 1-8.

But in order to understand Blake's feeling about Jesus properly, it is necessary that we should be careful to remember that, though he spent much of his energy in attacking existing institutions and ideas, he was a man with large and wonderful constructive ideals. It was indeed as a builder that he desired to be known; and it is significant of the judgment of time upon him that his best known lines are those in which he describes himself in the rôle of a builder:

> "I will not cease from mental fight,
>   Nor shall my sword sleep in my hand,
>   Till we have built Jerusalem
>   In England's green and pleasant land."

And perhaps the most beautiful passage in his writings is his description of the ideal city of his dreams:

> "Lo!
> The stones are Pity and the bricks well wrought Affections
> Enamelled by Love and Kindness; and the tiles engraven gold,
> Labour of merciful hands. The beams and rafters are Forgiveness;

The mortar and cement of the work, tears of Honesty;
    the nails
And the screws and the iron braces well-wrought Blan-
    dishments,
And well contrivéd words, firm-fixing, never forgotten,
Always comforting the remembrance; the floors,
    Humility;
The ceilings, Devotion; the hearths, Thanksgiving."

It was just because the "systems" of his day prevented
at every point the building of his ideal city that he attacked them. His destructive criticism was simply an
incident in what was to him a great, pressing, positive
task. And wheresoever in the wide world he heard of
men breaking the bonds of systems—political, religious,
or other—he lifted up his voice in exultation:

"He sent his two Servants, Whitfield and Wesley; were
    they Prophets,
Or were they Idiots or Madmen? Show us miracles!
Can you have greater Miracles than these? Men who
    devote
Their life's whole comfort to entire scorn and injury
    and death?"

Rebellion against outworn authority was to him one of
the credentials of holiness; and his heart warmed to any
man who, like Jesus, "suffered without the gate." When
the American colonies broke loose from the tyrannous
absolutism of Georgian England, Blake greatly rejoiced
and sang one of his great "prophecies." In "America" is
a song which is one of the classics of the literature of
liberty:

"The morning comes, the night decays, the watchmen leave
    their station,
The grave is burst, the spices shed, the linen wrappéd up;
The bones of death, the cov'ring clay, the sinews shrunk
    and dried

Reviving shake, inspiring move, breathing, awakening,
Spring like redeeméd captives, when their bonds and
bars are burst.
Let the slave grinding at the mill run out into the field,
Let him look up into the heavens and laugh in the
bright air;
Let the enchainéd soul, shut up in darkness and in sigh-
ing
Whose face has never seen a smile in thirty weary years,
Rise and look out; his chains are loose, his dungeon doors
are open,
And let his wife and children return from the oppressor's
scourge.
They look behind at every step, and believe it is a dream,
Singing, 'The Sun has left his blackness and has found
a fresher morning
And the fair Moon rejoices in the clear and cloudless
night;
For Empire is no more, and now the Lion and the Wolf
shall cease.' "

This kind of man, then, was William Blake. His passion
was to set men free from all hard and fast systems of
thought and conduct, so that the creative urge of personality, the divine in man, should express itself freely
and fully. Shelley pleaded for freedom because he had a
tender heart for suffering humanity; Blake fought for
freedom in order that every man might have the chance
to rise to the full stature of his manhood.

Fifth Week, Fourth Day

[And they went every man unto his own house: but
Jesus went unto the mount of Olives. And early in the
morning he came again into the temple, and all the people came unto him; and he sat down, and taught them.
And the scribes and the Pharisees bring a woman taken
in adultery; and having set her in the midst, they say
unto him, Master, this woman hath been taken in adultery,
in the very act. Now in the law Moses commanded us
to stone such: what then sayest thou of her? And this
they said, tempting him, that they might have whereof

to accuse him. But Jesus stooped down, and with his
finger wrote on the ground. But when they continued
asking him, he lifted up himself, and said unto them,
He that is without sin among you, let him first cast a
stone at her. And again he stooped down, and with his
finger wrote on the ground. And they, when they heard
it, went out one by one, beginning from the eldest, even
unto the last: and Jesus was left alone, and the woman,
where she was, in the midst. And Jesus lifted up himself, and said unto her, Woman, where are they? did no
man condemn thee? And she said, No man, Lord. And
Jesus said, Neither do I condemn thee: go thy way;
from henceforth sin no more.]—John 8: 1-11.

Perhaps the best instance we have of Blake's violent
assaults upon binding convention is to be found in his
poem called "The Everlasting Gospel." Here, in his own
characteristic way, he sets out to deny one by one the
characteristic features of the pulpit Christ of his day. His
exordium is a promise of stormy times to follow:

> "The vision of Christ that thou dost see
> Is my vision's greatest enemy . . .
> Thine is the friend of all mankind,
> Mine speaks in parables to the blind;
> Thine loves the same world that mine hates,
> Thy heaven doors are my hell-gates.
> Socrates taught what Meletus
> Loathed as a nation's bitterest curse;
> And Caiaphas was in his own mind
> A benefactor to mankind.
> Both read the Bible day and night,
> But thou read'st black where I read white."

Blake's vehemence often leads him, as it does here, to
indefensible and confusing extremes of statement. When
he assailed the conventional view of Jesus as "the friend
of all mankind," he was probably recalling the cleansing
of the temple and the denunciation of the Pharisees. The
"gentle Jesus, meek and mild," of current religion seemed
to Blake a mere caricature. He perceived that an undis-

criminating lenity was not a genuine feature of the gospel portrait; yet Jesus *was* "the friend of all mankind," and Blake seems not to have perceived that Jesus loved the very men he chastised.

In this forthright way, Blake proceeds to attack the outstanding characteristics of the popular Christ. Was Jesus gentle? Was he chaste? Was he humble? And he piles up the case against the pusillanimous, decorous, servile Jesus whom he supposed the contemporary pulpit preached. It is clear that these adjectives, *gentle, chaste, humble,* had for Blake an offensive meaning, else he would hardly have used them in his attack upon the current religion. Yet Jesus was gentle, chaste, and humble, in the strictest sense. But properly understood, in the Christian vocabulary gentleness does not mean *softness;* and chastity does not mean *prudishness,* while humility is not self-abasement, but *the mean between self-contempt and self-conceit.*

This undiscriminating vehemence of Blake robs his protests of much of the force they would otherwise have possessed. We see what he means; but the people whom he attacked would naturally use the manner and the matter of his speech against him; and would indeed be able to do so with a tolerable show of plausibility. Nevertheless, he understood the essential quality of Jesus far more clearly and told it far more vividly than the conventional Christian of his day. He smashed through the trappings which obscured the personal outlines of the man Jesus and fashioned a figure more convincing and attractive than the dull and uninteresting theological Christ of the eighteenth century.

Fifth Week, Fifth Day

Think not that I came to destroy the law or the prophets: I came not to destroy, but to fulfil. For verily I say unto you, Till heaven and earth pass away, one jot or one tittle shall in no wise pass away from the

law, till all things be accomplished. **Whosoever therefore shall break one of these least commandments, and
shall teach men so, shall be called least in the kingdom
of heaven: but whosoever shall do and teach them, he
shall be called great in the kingdom of heaven. For I
say unto you, that except your righteousness shall exceed
the righteousness of the scribes and Pharisees, ye shall
in no wise enter into the kingdom of heaven.—Matt.
5: 17-20.**

In that extraordinary production, "The Marriage of
Heaven and Hell," Blake says, *"Jesus was all virtue, and
acted from impulse, not from rules."* Here we have a
clue to Blake's criticism of the conventional picture of
Jesus.

In the fifth chapter of Matthew, Jesus, in quoting the
commandment "Thou shalt not murder," goes on to point
out that the spirit of this commandment forbade the anger
which leads to murder, and the offense which leads to
the anger. Similarly, He says that the commandment
which forbade the adulterous act also forbade the adulterous thought.

Now, men are apt to fall into the habit of supposing that
the provisions of law define their *moral* obligations. They
come to think that the whole duty of man is enclosed
within the letter of the law and this habit of emphasizing
the letter of the law is what we call *legalism.* The classic
representatives of this spirit were the Pharisees and
Scribes of the New Testament; and what Jesus does in
the fifth of Matthew is to show that the spirit of the law
must and does go far beyond the letter. But the letter
of the law acts as a curb upon the true spirit of moral
goodness. This spirit is essentially an original and creative thing. It is, to use Blake's word, an impulse. It is
something which is forever trying to outdo its own best.
It recognizes no limits to its scope. It does not break
the law, but transcends it, though to a narrow mind it
sometimes seems to break the law, as Jesus seemed to do
when He healed on the Sabbath Day.

This was what Blake perceived. He said that men supposed moral goodness to be an affair of observing a code of rules; and he said that Jesus insisted that the code of rules was a smaller thing than the inward spirit of goodness and that it tended to imprison the moral impulse. The law is good so far as it goes, it shows the way; but when we regard it as a terminal, as a complete summary of moral right, then it becomes an evil.

But Blake saw more than this. He saw that just as the Scribes and Pharisees exalted the letter of the law of Moses, so the preachers and teachers of his time treated the words of Jesus with a literalism which converted them into a new law; that is, Jesus Himself had come to be treated in the very way against which He protested in the case of Moses. A Christian legalism had superseded the Jewish, with the same results. The Gospel of grace had become a hard system of law, with prohibitions and punishments. In the Fourth Book of "Jerusalem," he sees a "wheel of fire" which devoured "all things in its loud fury and devouring course" and was told it was "the wheel of religion."

"I wept and said,—is this the law of Jesus,
This terrible devouring sword turned every way?
He answered: Jesus died because He strove
Against the current of this Wheel: its name is
Caiaphas, the dark Preacher of Death,
Of sin, of sorrow, and of punishment:
Opposing Nature! It is Natural Religion;[1]
But Jesus is the bright Preacher of Life,
Creating Nature from this fiery Law,
By self-denial and Forgiveness of Sin.
Go therefore, cast out devils in Christ's name,
Heal the sick of spiritual disease,
Pity the evil; for thou art not sent

[1] *Natural religion* as contrasted with *revealed* religion. This is a reference to eighteenth century deism, which was an attempt to eliminate the element of supernatural revelation from religion. This was, of course, anathema to Blake, to whom revelation was the supreme reality.

> To smite with terror and with punishments
> Those who are sick, like to the Pharisees,
> Crucifying and encompassing sea and land
> For proselytes to tyranny and wrath.
> But to the publicans and harlots go.
> Teach them true happiness, but let no curse
> Go out of thy mouth to blight their peace.
> For Hell is opened to Heaven; thine eyes behold
> The dungeons burst, and the prisoners set free."

Law works through judgment and punishment; Blake saw
that the Gospel worked through judgment and mercy. It
does not condone sin; but its remedy for it is forgiveness.
It allows moral evil to reap its harvest of sorrow; but
it conquers it by mercy. And it was to restore to Christianity its true character as the Gospel of grace and mercy
that Blake labored so passionately, in contrast to the arid
and respectable legalism that passed for Christianity in
his day.

Fifth Week, Sixth Day

**And he said unto his disciples, It is impossible but that
occasions of stumbling should come: but woe unto him,
through whom they come! It were well for him if a
millstone were hanged about his neck, and he were
thrown into the sea, rather than that he should cause one
of these little ones to stumble. Take heed to yourselves:
if thy brother sin, rebuke him; and if he repent, forgive
him. And if he sin against thee seven times in the day,
and seven times turn again to thee, saying, I repent; thou
shall forgive him.—Luke 17: 1-4.**

"Let men be free to be their own true selves" is Blake's
version of the Gospel. Emancipate them from the tyranny
of Reason and Desire within and from legalism and
dogmatism without. Let the creative impulse go free,
creating what it will.

And one thing it will create is a society. Free men
will instinctively swing to the pole of brotherhood. It
was as the embodiment of this society-creating impulse

that Jesus stood out most prominently in Blake's mind. He sees Him as the teacher of brotherhood:

"Jesus said, 'Wouldst thou love one who never died
For thee, or ever die for one who had not died for thee?
And if God dieth not for Man and giveth not himself
Eternally for Man, Man could not exist; for Man is Love
As God is Love: every kindness to another is a little Death
In the Divine Image, nor can Man exist but by Brotherhood."

But Jesus is more than teacher; He is the living core of this brotherhood.

"He who would see the Divinity must see Him in His Children,
One first, in friendship and love; then a Divine Family and in the midst
Jesus will appear; and so he who wishes to see a Vision, a perfect Whole,
Must see it in its Minute Particulars."

Blake is fond of this expression, the "Minute Particular"; and by it he means the single soul, the unit of life. He saw men engaged in making great abstract generalizations and calling them laws; but, he says, It is not laws that matter but men. Every

"Particular is a Man, a Divine Member of the Divine Jesus."

And he goes on:

"Labour well the Minute Particulars; attend to the Little Ones";

and here is the heart of his ethics:

"He who would do good to another must do it in Minute Particulars.
General good is the plea of the scoundrel, hypocrite, and flatterer."

This is surely bedrock, a real fixed point for thought and conduct. True reverence for and a right relation to the living man, my neighbor—here is the law and the prophets.

For Blake, then, morality is the art of fellowship; and the virtues he extols are the society-making graces. It is from this that his continual emphasis on forgiveness comes. "The Spirit of Jesus," he says, "is continual forgiveness of sins." And again, "The Glory of Christianity is to conquer by forgiveness."

"Why should punishment weave the veil with iron wheels
    of war
  When forgiveness might weave it with wings of Cheru-
    bim?"

The law of God for human life is reciprocity, mutuality —call it what you will. In a world where men need and cannot do without each other, where separation spells starvation of spirit, the tempers and policies which sunder men spring from a kind of atheism. Instead of the healing and unitive influences which should produce the society of his dreams, Blake saw the world overrun with passions of vengeance, doctrines of punishment, which, while they were supposed to repress the evil in the world, deepened and widened the gulf which divides man from his fellow. Our human frailty makes it impossible for us to live together except upon a basis of mutual forbearance and forgiveness. The true life is that which makes for human brotherhood. That man has found himself who has learned to bind his brother-man to his heart in healing, forgiving, long-suffering love.

Fifth Week, Seventh Day

And I lifted up mine eyes, and saw, and behold a man with a measuring line in his hand. Then said I, Whither goest thou? And he said unto me, To measure Jerusalem, to see what is the breadth thereof, and what is the length thereof. And, behold, the angel that talked with

me went forth, and another angel went out to meet him,
and said unto him, Run, speak to this young man, saying,
Jerusalem shall be inhabited as villages without walls,
by reason of the multitude of men and cattle therein.
For I, saith the Lord, will be unto her a wall of fire
round about, and I will be the glory in the midst of her.
—Zech. 2 : 1-5.

To Blake then, Jesus was the core, the heart of an
expanding fellowship of redeemed men. Dante saw Him
as the central glory of the host of the redeemed in heaven;
but Blake's vision is in an earthly setting. He sees Jerusalem arising in England, in the world; and it is to be a
Jerusalem like Zechariah's, a Jerusalem without walls—
so full of life, so irresistibly expanding that no walls can
contain it:

> "In my Exchanges every land
>   Shall walk; and mine in every land
>   Mutual shall build Jerusalem
>   Both heart in heart and hand in hand."

This is assuredly the "League of Nations." But Blake
sees that it is only to be realized as nations as well as individuals practice fellowship. The old doctrines of sovereignty and empire must give way to an ideal of reciprocity
and cooperation. To the jingo patriotism of his own
country, Blake addressed a pointed question:

> "Is this thy soft family love,
>   Thy cruel patriarchal pride,
>   Planting thy family alone,
>   Destroying all the world beside?"

The question has not lost its pertinence; indeed it has
today a wider challenge. Imperialism, Chauvinism, Pan-
Germanism—all these things and such as these are of their
father the devil.

Naturally Blake detested all forms of militarism.

"The strongest poison ever known
 Came from Cæsar's royal crown;
 Nought can deform the human race
 Like to the armour's iron brace.
 When gold and gems adorn the plough
 To peaceful arts shall Envy bow."

And he has much to say on this subject in the same spirit. But this attitude in Blake's mind was the very reverse of a soft passivity. He was a fighting man; his images are chiefly borrowed from the battlefield. To him, the fighting instinct was a priceless gift of God; and its tragedy as he saw it was that it had been misdirected. Greedy men had exploited it for selfish ends. It was muddied and soiled by the spirit of hate, of revenge, or destruction. But to suppose that there is no way of satisfying the fighting instinct save by the slaughter and destruction of men was, to Blake, mere foolishness. He was no pacifist in the sense of desiring peace above all things else; what he wanted and was ready to fight for was not peace, but fellowship. But that sort of fighting requires peculiar weapons.

"Our wars are wars of life, and wounds of love,
 With intellectual spears and longwinged arrows of
   thought,
 Mutual in one another's wrath, all renewing
 We live as One Man. For contracting our infinite senses
 We behold multitude; or expanding, we behold as One,
 As one man all the Universal Family; and that man
 We call Jesus the Christ, and He in us, and we in Him,
 Live in perfect harmony in Eden the land of life,
 Giving, receiving, and forgiving each other's trespasses."

Here, then, it is that Blake places Jesus. He is the Incarnation and Embodiment of the Divine Spirit of fellowship, the source and the channel of the divine-human impulse that makes for fellowship. He is the Soul of the Universal Family, He is the supreme manifestation of the creative urge of God which expresses itself in many ways, but chiefly and most gloriously in the creative evolution of that society of man which is also the Kingdom of God.

SUGGESTIONS FOR THOUGHT AND DISCUSSION

Can you distinguish between Religion and Theology and between Morality and Law? Which do you think more important, a living religion or a sound theology? What is meant by the statement that "the maximum of legal obligation is the minimum of moral obligation"?

Do you think William Blake was right in insisting that the chief end of man was to be creative?

What is William Blake's message to our time?

It has been said that salvation meant to Zacchæus being made a member of a family, his inclusion in a society; and Zacchæus himself felt it to be so, for he began at once to do certain *social* acts. Read the story of Zacchæus and consider it in the light of Blake's view of Jesus.

What are the "society-making virtues"?

CHAPTER VI

The Poet as Philosopher— Browning

(1812—1889)

We saw that it was Browning's view that if Shelley had lived, he would have become a Christian. It may be that Browning recognized in Shelley's mind a certain kinship with his own and felt that he might in time have come to share his own faith. At least it is true that what we see as tendencies in Shelley have reached the point of a robust faith in Browning. It is true we cannot trace very clearly the early stages of the movement of Browning's thought into the faith of his poetry; in any case, it is doubtful whether it is possible to give a systematic account of Browning's mental development. He did not reach this faith altogether by processes of reasoning. "I know," he once wrote, "I have myself been aware of the communication of something more subtle than a ratiocinative process, when the convictions of 'genius' have thrilled my soul to its depths." That is to say, things *came* to him. He did not indeed despise reasoning processes; nor was he like Blake in his fear of reason; but he knew there were other avenues into truth than those of accurate logic. Browning's faith does, however, stand out as a coherent whole, of which it is possible to give a fairly complete account within narrow limits.

Shelley and Blake were products of an age of revolution, and we have seen the emphasis they laid on liberty.

Browning, like his contemporary Tennyson, also reflects an age of revolution, but of a different kind. It was revolution in the region of thought. The great advance of scientific knowledge had disintegrated many of the accepted beliefs; and it seemed as if the very foundations of life itself had been unsettled. Some idea of the character of the age in which Browning and Tennyson lived can be gathered from the circumstance that Charles Darwin was a contemporary of both; and that "The Origin of Species," Darwin's great epoch-making work, appeared in 1859, thirty years before Browning's death and thirty-three before Tennyson's. It was also the age of the great agnostics, Huxley, Spencer, and Tyndall, who declared that no knowledge was reliable except that reached by the scientific method, and since God could not be reached in that way, it was useless and futile to suppose that anything could be known about Him. It was a period of great intellectual uncertainty and unrest; but Browning and Tennyson weathered the gale and reached the port of a living faith. Tennyson presents us with the figure of a sad but eager seeker, winning his way into faith with somewhat hesitating steps; but Browning seems rather the strong man fighting his own way through the smoke and tumult of battle into the clear air beyond.

DAILY READINGS

Sixth Week, First Day

For this commandment which I command thee this day, it is not too hard for thee, neither is it far off. It is not in heaven, that thou shouldest say, Who shall go up for us to heaven, and bring it unto us, and make us to hear it, that we may do it? Neither is it beyond the sea, that thou shouldest say, Who shall go over the sea for us, and bring it unto us, and make us to hear it, that we may do it? But the word is very nigh unto thee, in thy mouth, and in thy heart, that thou mayest do it.—Deut. 30: 11-14.

Like Shelley, Browning sees that behind all things there

is some one ultimate Reality of which they are but the manifestations. This is God,

> "From whom all being emanates; all power
> Proceeds; in whom is life for evermore,
> Yet whom existence in its lowest form
> Includes. . . .   He dwells in all
> From life's minute beginnings, up at last
> To man—the consummation of this scheme
> Of being; the completion of this sphere
> Of life."

This language is capable of a pantheistic interpretation —pantheism being the view that there is no other God than the totality of all things. But Browning was not a pantheist. For though he was a strong believer in the divine immanence, he did not identify God with the universe as the pantheists did. The pantheists said, God is everything that is; but Browning said, God is *in* everything that is. And this did not prevent him from believing that God was also above and independent of the universe.

> "Choice of the world, choice of the thing I am,
> Both emanate alike from Thy dread play
> Of operation *outside* this our sphere,"

says the Pope in "The Ring and the Book"; and the view is Browning's own. God immanent—that is, *God in us*— and God transcendent—that is, *God over us*—both these ideas are necessary to a full doctrine of God. It may not be easy to harmonize these two thoughts into a single conception; but that is simply because our minds are not capable of enclosing within themselves realities which are in their nature infinite. We cannot comprehend God; the best we can do is to apprehend Him dimly, and the forms under which we express our thought of God are only approximations. They are the best we can do; and they are never complete, never final.

Man was, however, made in the divine image; and that implies a sufficiently close kinship between the divine nature and the human to make it possible for man to apprehend in some degree the self-revelation of God.

"O Thou as represented here to me
　In such conception as my soul allows,
　Under thy measureless, my atom width. . . .
Existent, somewhere, somehow, as a whole;
Here, as a whole proportioned to our sense,—
There (which is nowhere, speech must babble thus!)
In the absolute immensity, the whole
Appreciable solely by Thyself,—
Here, by the little mind of man, reduced
To littleness that suits his faculty."

Sixth Week, Second Day

Being therefore justified by faith, let us have peace with God through our Lord Jesus Christ; through whom also we have had our access by faith into this grace wherein we stand; and let us rejoice in hope of the glory of God. And not only so, but let us also rejoice in our tribulations: knowing that tribulation worketh patience; and patience, probation; and probation, hope: and hope putteth not to shame; because the love of God hath been shed abroad in our hearts through the Holy Ghost which was given unto us. For while we were yet weak, in due season Christ died for the ungodly. For scarcely for a righteous man will one die: for peradventure for the good man some one would even dare to die. But God commendeth his own love toward us, in that, while we were yet sinners, Christ died for us.—Rom. 5: 1-8.

Man then can only apprehend God in "littleness that suits his faculty"; yet he need never know less of God than what he needs to live by. Something of God he may discover in himself, and something in nature; and this is a good deal.

"Conjecture of the Worker by the work?
　Is there strength there? Enough. Intelligence?

Ample; but goodness in a like degree?
Not to the human eye in the present state."

And Browning goes on to compare the revelation of
God in the universe to an isosceles triangle, the two
equal sides of which, *strength* and *intelligence,* are clear
enough; but the base of which, *goodness,* is not in sight.

Nothing did more to unsettle man's faith in God than
the revelation of the fierce and bloody struggle for survival
which science had discovered in its study of nature; and
this is what Browning is referring to here when he says
that goodness is less apparent in nature than intelligence
and power. We know now, as the contemporaries of Darwin did not, that survival in nature is at least as much
a matter of cooperation as of struggle; but Browning had
to seek evidence of the divine goodness elsewhere. Where
is the base of the triangle to be found?

Browning finds it in Jesus. The story of Jesus com-
pletes God's revelation of Himself. This "tale" of God
"in the world's mouth" supplies the "instance"

"Of love without a limit. So is strength,
    So is intelligence; let love be so,
    Unlimited in its self-sacrifice,
    Then is the tale true and God shows complete."

This, in Browning's view, is the meaning of Jesus. He
is supremely the manifestation of the divine love; and
because He is this, He is the key to all the perplexing
problems which the universe presents. Our poet believed
what he makes the dying apostle say:

"I say, the acknowledgment of God in Christ
    Accepted by thy reason, solves for thee
    All questions in the earth and out of it."

To Browning, therefore, Jesus is the clue to the universe
and to life. He is the base of the triangle, the revelation
of that infinite love upon which all things rest. Shelley

had to believe in an almightiness of love as the basis of all life; but in his case, it was a blind act of faith required by his philosophy. In Browning's case, however, this faith rests upon a reading of the story of Jesus.

Sixth Week, Third Day

Let not your heart be troubled: ye believe in God, believe also in me. In my Father's house are many mansions; if it were not so, I would have told you; for I go to prepare a place for you. And if I go and prepare a place for you, I come again, and will receive you unto myself; that where I am, there ye may be also. And whither I go, ye know the way. Thomas saith unto him, Lord, we know not whither thou goest; how know we the way? Jesus saith unto him, I am the way, and the truth, and the life: no one cometh unto the Father, but by me. If ye had known me, ye would have known my Father also: from henceforth ye know him, and have seen him.—John 14: 1-7.

We should do Browning less than justice, however, if we supposed that he regarded Jesus merely as a factor which helped him to work out his philosophy. The figure of Jesus had to our poet a very definite personal significance. He has no patience with the critics who seek to whittle Jesus down so as to make Him fit into their own private categories; or those whose methods of analysis prevent them from seeing the wood for the trees, who lose the figure of Jesus in the details of analysis. He expresses some considerable impatience with the tendency in the study of the gospels to lay too heavy an emphasis on

"the ineptitude of the time
And the penman's prejudice,"

a process which having "strained and abated" the story

"Of foreign matter, left, for residuum
A Man !—a right true man, however,
Whose work was worthy a man's endeavour."

97

To leave a "man" in the story is indeed more than some critics have done; but even this, says Browning,

> "leaves you—vacuity.
> Thus much of Christ does he reject?
> And what retain? His intellect?
> What is it I must reverence duly?
> Poor intellect for worship truly,
> Which leaves me simply what was told
>   (If mere morality, bereft
>   Of the God in Christ, be all that's left)
> Elsewhere by voices manifold. . . .
> Christ's goodness, then—does that fare better?
> Strange goodness, which upon the score
>   Of being goodness, the mere due
> Of man to fellow-man, much more
>   To God—should take another view
> Of its possessor's privilege
> And bid him rule his race!"

The poet does not believe that the supremacy of Jesus could rest on His morality, though

> "Morality to the uttermost
>   Supreme in Christ, we all confess."

It rests upon His own person, as He himself claimed:

> "Does the precept run—'Believe in good,
>   In justice, truth, now understood
>   For the first time'? or—'Believe in me
>   Who lived and died, yet essentially
>   Am Lord of Life'?"

Browning was ready to accept Jesus at His own estimate of Himself. Jesus is not only the clue to a true view of the universe; He is the Christ, who enters into personal relations with men and brings them to fulness of life.

Sixth Week, Fourth Day

He that receiveth you receiveth me, and he that receiveth me receiveth him that sent me. He that receiveth

a prophet in the name of a prophet shall receive a
prophet's reward; and he that receiveth a righteous man
in the name of a righteous man shall receive a righteous
man's reward.   And whosoever shall give to drink unto
one of these little ones a cup of cold water only, in the
name of a disciple, verily I say unto you, he shall in
no wise lose his reward.—Matt. 10: 40-42.

A faith is known by its fruits; and if a faith is validated
by the hope it kindles, then Browning's faith stands justified.   Browning had too true an eye not to recognize the
tragedy of which our life is so full; but his faith enables
him to see in the brokenness and imperfection of human
life not a reason for despair, but the very ground of hope
for men's future.   Man is not in a state of being so much
as of becoming.   Progress is

> "Man's distinctive mark alone,
> Not God's and not the beasts': God is, they are,
> Man partly is and wholly hopes to be."

All man's striving is but the evidence of his unrealized
destiny; and if he falls and stumbles on the upward way,
what of that?   Of the failures and brokenness of life
Browning has two important things to tell us:
First, that we are judged not by what we achieve but
by what we mean and try to achieve.   The great passage
from "Rabbi Ben Ezra" is well known:

> "Not on the vulgar mass
> Called 'work' must sentence pass,
> Things done, that took the eye and had the price. . . .
>
> But all, the world's coarse thumb
> And finger failed to plumb,
> So passed in making up the main account;
> All instincts immature,
> All purposes unsure,
> That weighed not as his work, yet swelled the man's
> amount.

Thoughts hardly to be packed
Into a narrow act,
Fancies that broke through language and escaped;
    All I could never be,
    All, men ignored in me,
This, I was worth to God whose wheel the pitcher shaped."

And in "Saul" he puts the same thing in another way:

" 'Tis not what man does which exalts him, but what man
    would do."

This is, of course, only the doctrine of justification by
faith put in a modern idiom. For faith is at bottom an
attitude of the soul, or, to quote Dr. Du Bose once more,
"the entire disposition of our entire selves God-ward,
holiness-ward." We are set right before God when we
set ourselves Godward. Justification is by attitude and
not by achievement. God accepts us for what we desire
and long to be. He judges us not by what we accomplish,
but by what we *would* accomplish. Of course He can
know what we *would* accomplish, only by what we *try*
to accomplish; and even if we fail, even then failure is
as good as success so far as our relation to God is concerned. It is not the deed that God looks upon, but the
intention and the motive. The workmen who went into
the vineyard at the eleventh hour got a whole day's pay,
because they had been willing to work all day if someone
had hired them. He who receives a prophet in the name
of a prophet shall receive a prophet's reward. He may
have no prophetic gift and may never utter a prophetic
word, but just because he gives bed and board to a
prophet simply because he is a prophet, he shows the kind
of company he wishes to keep. That is where he desires
to belong; and God counts him as belonging there. We
are judged not by the great things we say or do, but by
the company we keep, the purposes we cherish, the kind
of universe in which we desire to live. That is a comfort.

Sixth Week, Fifth Day

But we have this treasure in earthen vessels, that the exceeding greatness of the power may be of God, and not from ourselves; we are pressed on every side, yet not straitened; perplexed, yet not unto despair; pursued, yet not forsaken; smitten down, yet not destroyed; always bearing about in the body the dying of Jesus, that the life also of Jesus may be manifested in our body. For we which live are alway delivered unto death for Jesus' sake, that the life also of Jesus may be manifested in our mortal flesh. So then death worketh in us, but life in you. But having the same spirit of faith, according to that which is written, I believed, and therefore did I speak; we also believe, and therefore also we speak; knowing that he which raised up the Lord Jesus shall raise up us also with Jesus, and shall present us with you. For all things are for your sakes, that the grace, being multiplied through the many, may cause the thanksgiving to abound unto the glory of God.

Wherefore we faint not; but though our outward man is decaying, yet our inward man is renewed day by day. For our light affliction, which is for the moment, worketh for us more and more exceedingly an eternal weight of glory; while we look not at the things which are seen, but at the things which are not seen: for the things which are seen are temporal; but the things which are not seen are eternal.—II Cor. 4: 7-18.

The second important thing Browning has to tell us of our human failures is the sequel of the first. It is that our honest failures are really guarantees of final success.

"And what is our failure here but a triumph's evidence
    For the fulness of the days? Have we withered or
        agonised?
  Why else was the pause prolonged but that singing
        might issue thence?
  Why rushed the discords in but that harmony should be
        prized?"

This is the theme of the great poem called "Abt Vogler." Yet though Browning is so sure of our ultimate triumph, he does not see us achieving it wholly in the world of time. We are moving onward; of this our falls and failures assure us. But the goal is not here.

> "Life is a probation and the earth no goal
>   But starting point of man."

Our perfect destiny lies beyond the veil. The poet's faith in the future life was due to his sense of the sheer indestructibility of that strange and wonderful thing, *personality;* and since personality may not achieve its fulness here, well then, it is awaiting it over there.

> "There shall never be one lost good! What was, shall live as before,
>   The evil is null, is nought, is silence implying sound;
>   What was good shall be good, with, for evil, so much good more;
>   On the earth the broken arcs; in the heaven, a perfect round."

This sane, unyielding optimism Browning derived from his sense of the meaning of Jesus. God revealed in Christ is essential Love; and that meant that, as Pippa sang,

> "God's in his heaven—
>   All's right with the world!"

but it meant no less that

> "The mightiness of love was curled
>   Inextricably round about"

all the life and process of the world. Love underlies and governs the movement of all things; and in a world thus governed, it is always the best that ultimately happens.

Sixth Week, Sixth Day

God, having of old time spoken unto the fathers in the prophets by divers portions and in divers manners, hath at the end of these days spoken unto us in his Son, whom

he appointed heir of all things, through whom also he
made the worlds; who being the effulgence of his glory,
and the very image of his substance, and upholding all
things by the word of his power, when he had made
purification of sins, sat down on the right hand of the
Majesty on high.—Heb. 1: 1-3.

What was it in Christ that suggested to Browning this
stupendous meaning? We shall probably discover the
answer to this question most readily in the poem "Saul."
David in this poem "is occupied with no speculative question, but with the practical problem of saving a ruined
soul." He sweeps the universe and his own soul in quest
of healing for the King. But it is all in vain. Then he
turns to God. He had himself been willing to give his
soul for Saul's redemption. Was this love that prompted
him to this willing self-sacrifice less than God's?

"Do I find love so full in my nature, God's ultimate gift,
 That I doubt His own love can compete with it?"

David had the love to do what he wished for Saul; but
he lacked the power. But God had the power as well as
the love.

"Would I suffer for Him that I love? So wouldst thou
   —so wilt thou!
 So shall crown thee the topmost, ineffablest, uttermost
   crown,
 And thy love fill infinitude wholly, nor leave up nor down
 One spot for the creature to stand in."

David reads his own love into God's heart—the love which
gave the gift of love to man must be of a piece with what
it gives. What man's love would do, God's love would
assuredly do—and more. When J. M. Barrie says that the
God that little boys say their prayers to has a face very
much like their mother's, he is only putting David's argument in another way. David seeks and finds his flesh in
the Godhead.

> "O Saul, it shall be
A Face like my face that receives thee; a Man like to me,
Thou shalt love and be loved by, for ever: a Hand like this hand
Shall throw open the gates of new life to thee! See the Christ stand!"

David apprehends the eternal humanity of God; and it was this eternal humanity that, according to Browning, came into the world in the person of Jesus. The Incarnation is the necessary sequel to the poet's thought of God. Since it is God's will to reveal Himself to man, and since He made man in His own image, His perfect revelation must be through and in a man, if man is to understand it. And so the "Word became flesh and dwelt among us."

It is hardly necessary to add that Browning finds the crowning point of Jesus' story in His death; here is that unlimited self-sacrifice which shows "love without a limit." Calvary was that

> "transcendent act
Beside which even the creation fades
Into a puny exercise of power."

Sixth Week, Seventh Day

For this cause we also, since the day we heard it, do not cease to pray and make request for you, that ye may be filled with the knowledge of his will in all spiritual wisdom and understanding, to walk worthily of the Lord unto all pleasing, bearing fruit in every good work, and increasing in the knowledge of God; strengthened with all power, according to the might of his glory, unto all patience and longsuffering with joy; giving thanks unto the Father, who made us meet to be partakers of the inheritance of the saints in light; who delivered us out of the power of darkness, and translated us into the kingdom of the Son of his love; in whom we have our redemption, the forgiveness of our sins: who is the image of the invisible God, the firstborn of all creation; for in him were all things created, in the heavens and upon the earth, things visible and things invisible, whether thrones or dominions or principalities or powers; all things have

been created through him, and unto him; and he is before all things, and in him all things consist. And he is
the head of the body, the church: who is the beginning,
the firstborn from the dead; that in all things he might
have the preeminence. For it was the good pleasure
of the Father that in him should all the fulness dwell;
and through him to reconcile all things unto himself,
having made peace through the blood of his cross.—
Col. 1: 9-20.

While the Incarnation has thus its larger place and
meaning in the sum of things, the love of God in Christ
has also a personal significance for the individual. It
is the assurance of mercy for the contrite, and the promise
of the soul's salvation. "Saul the mistake, Saul the failure" may put his trust in Christ; but Browning is not
forgetful that unrepented evil must make Christ other
than Saviour. "John, the Master of the Temple of God,"
was being burnt in Paris for his misdeeds and in his
extremity calls on Christ. But it is not the cry of a
penitent:

"So as John called now through the fire amain
    On the Name he had cursed with, all his life—
To the Person he had bought and sold again—
    For the Face, with his daily buffets rife—
Feature by feature, It took its place,
    And his voice like a mad dog's choking bark,
At the steady whole of the Judge's face—
    Died. Forth John's soul flared into the dark."

The tragedy of impenitence is that it turns the merciful
Saviour into the unrelenting Judge.

But this is not "the face of Jesus Christ" which Browning saw for himself. It is another; and its true parallel
is to be found in the writings of St. Paul.

Does Browning find in Jesus the clue to a satisfying
account of the universe? So does St. Paul; for "in Him,"
he says, "are all the treasures of wisdom and knowledge
hidden."

Does Browning see in Christ the crown and destiny of all things in the universe and out of it? No less does St. Paul, who declares that God purposed "to sum up all things in Christ, the things in the heavens, and the things upon the earth."

Does Browning find in Christ the fulfilment of the personal life? So also does St. Paul, who cried out, "I live; and yet no longer I, but Christ liveth in me."

Shall we wonder, then, that Browning should have so seen Jesus that he says of His face:

> "That one Face, far from vanish, rather grows,
>   Or decomposes but to recompose,
>   Become my universe that feels and knows"?

SUGGESTIONS FOR THOUGHT AND DISCUSSION

Why should the conception of evolution have unsettled men's faith?

The expression "the eternal humanity of God" has been used in this week's discussion. Is this a true conception, and how does it bear on the statement that "God made man in His own image"?

Discuss the interpretation of "justification by faith" given in the Fourth Day's reading.

Collect the New Testament passages in which the coming and death of Jesus are used to prove God's love; and compare them with Browning's view.

CHAPTER VII

The Poet as Seeker—Tennyson

(1809—1892)

Tennyson, as we have seen, lived in a time of intellectual unrest. New knowledge had shaken old beliefs. The Darwinian theory of evolution in particular seemed to contradict the traditional view of God as an all-powerful and benevolent Creator. All honest men who were not blinded by prejudice recognized that it was necessary to reexamine the foundations of faith, and that no good purpose was served by merely assailing the new knowledge and what seemed to be implied in it. Some indeed went farther and believed that increase of knowledge would not destroy the essence of faith, however it might require that the *forms* of faith should be modified. There was, so they held, a strong presumption that when the smoke of the conflict had cleared away, it would be found that the old faith would absorb the new knowledge and be itself revived and enriched.

But this position made it impossible for them to accept the growing view that the only valid knowledge was that reached by the senses and reasoning processes. A school arose which claimed that the scientific method was the adequate and sole avenue to truth; and what truth was not thus ascertained was unreliable. To this opinion Tennyson did not assent. He held that there were some things which were true which yet could not be *proved;* and these things are to be *believed.* And, "believing where he could not prove," Tennyson did not relinquish the foothold of faith.

Some of his great contemporaries, however, came to profess agnosticism. Since, they argued, it is impossible to demonstrate scientifically anything about God, or even to prove His existence, let us say frankly that we do not know. To many people this appeared to be the only honest way out of the difficulty; and so set in the age of agnosticism.

But Tennyson did not succumb to this pressure, though he felt the weight of it.

> "If e'er when faith had fallen asleep
>   I heard a voice 'Believe no more,'
>   And heard an ever-breaking shore
> That tumbled in the godless deep,
>
> A warmth within the breast would melt
>   The freezing reason's colder part,
>   And like a man in wrath the heart
> Stood up and answered, I have felt."

Tennyson would not have feeling usurp the place of reason, as reason tended to usurp the legitimate place of feeling. He would have each be in its own place doing its own work.

Tennyson, therefore, stands between the old faith and the new knowledge; and he is peculiarly the poet of reconciliation. He tries to bind the old and the new in a fresh, living whole. He does not, indeed, succeed; but this is a task in which no man has ever succeeded. It is a task which has to be carried on all the time; we have to do it in our own day. And Tennyson supplies us with the figure of the patient seeker, which is a true type of the living Christian thinker.

When inquiries were addressed to Tennyson concerning his view of Jesus, the poet would say to his son, "Answer them that I have given my belief in 'In Memoriam.'" "In Memoriam" was Tennyson's elegy upon the death of his friend, Arthur Hallam, and is his best known and best loved long work. Our present purpose need not lead us much farther afield, therefore, than this poem.[1]

DAILY READINGS

Seventh Week, First Day

And they come to Jericho: and as he went out from Jericho, with his disciples and a great multitude, the son of Timæus, Bartimæus, a blind beggar, was sitting by the way side. And when he heard that it was Jesus of Nazareth, he began to cry out, and say, Jesus, thou son of David, have mercy on me. And many rebuked him, that he should hold his peace: but he cried out the more a great deal, Thou son of David, have mercy on me. And Jesus stood still, and said, Call ye him. And they call the blind man, saying unto him, Be of good cheer: rise, he calleth thee. And he, casting away his garment, sprang up, and came to Jesus. And Jesus answered him, and said, What wilt thou that I should do unto thee? And the blind man said unto him, Rabboni, that I may receive my sight. And Jesus said unto him, Go thy way; thy faith hath made thee whole. And straightway he received his sight, and followed him in the way.—Mark 10: 46-52.

Tennyson was largely moved by the evidence which science had produced of the contradiction between the God who seemed to be revealed in nature and the God in whom he had been taught to believe. The God of his youth was kindly, friendly; and "not a sparrow fell to the ground without our Father." But nature seemed in the new light so callous, so careless of life, whether of the single life or of the type; and in particular did this shake the poet's faith in immortality. The blow left him staggering:

> "I falter where I firmly trod,
>   And falling with my weight of cares
>   Upon the great world's altar-stairs
> That slope through darkness up to God,

---

[1] The prose quotations from Tennyson in our study are taken from his biography written by his son, Hallam, second Lord Tennyson.

> I stretch lame hands of faith, and grope,
>   And gather dust and chaff, and call
>   To what I feel is Lord of all,
> And faintly trust the larger hope."

This is the point from which we start out with Tennyson. He fully accepted the scientific view of the world. "The physical world," says Professor Sedgwick, speaking of the poet, "is always the world as known to us through physical senses; the scientific view of it dominates his thought about it; and his general acceptance of this view is real and sincere, even when he utters the intensest feeling of its inadequacy to satisfy our deepest needs." He saw, as his scientific contemporaries saw,

> "Nature, red in tooth and claw
>   With ravine,"

shrieking against the belief that God is love. The "struggle for existence" and the "survival of the fittest," then the new scientific catchwords, had drenched nature in red blood. All this naturally led to the conclusion in some minds that no moral quality could belong to God. He was at the best a non-moral artificer, who had set this scheme of things at work and was indifferent to the cost of its working. But Tennyson refused to settle down to this stoical indifference, which seemed to many to be the only possible logical temper under the circumstances. "Behold," he cries,

> "Behold, we know not anything;
>   I can but trust that good shall fall
>   At last—far off—at last to all,
> And every winter change to spring."

Science should not and could not extinguish the poet's hope; and this hope sprang from the faith he clung to, that even yet the goodness of the spirit of the universe would be shown.

But when Tennyson said, "Behold, we know not anything," he was speaking within the circle of pure science. About the future, about God, about human destiny, science tells us nothing that is certain.   The scientist may if he choose trust

> "that somehow good
> Will be the final goal of ill,"

but further than this, by the help of his science alone, he cannot go.

Seventh Week, Second Day

Be not ashamed therefore of the testimony of our Lord, nor of me his prisoner: but suffer hardship with the gospel according to the power of God; who saved us, and called us with a holy calling, not according to our works, but according to his own purpose and grace, which was given us in Christ Jesus before times eternal, but hath now been manifested by the appearing of our Saviour Christ Jesus, who abolished death, and brought life and incorruption to light through the gospel.—II Tim. 1: 8-10.

There was one great omission in the thought of the scientific agnostics of the nineteenth century.   While they were studying nature, they did not give enough attention to the fact that man was also a part of nature; and that human intuitions and instincts are as important for a full understanding of nature as chemical reactions or physiological processes.

Now Tennyson found himself believing in God; and for him this instinctive feeling for God was a fact of enormous importance.   How came man to believe in God at all, if God Himself had not been there to call out the belief?   And, indeed, belief in the "self-conscious personality of God" came to appear to him to be "the backbone of the world."   Like Browning and all of us, he admitted that God could not be known in "His whole

world-self and all in all"; yet "I believe," he said, "that
God reveals Himself in each individual soul." And here,
in the witness of our highest intuitions to God, Tennyson
found a range of facts which helped him to reconstruct
his faith in the face of the destructive witness of science.
That God is love is a belief which, according to our poet,
we get "from ourselves, from the highest within us."
Observe here the difference between Tennyson and
Browning. Tennyson recovers his faith from an inquiry
into his own soul; Browning has to recover it from
something outside himself—in the witness of the story of
Jesus to the love of God. From this point we shall be
led to another of importance in comparing these two poets.

It was, however, in his thought about immortality that
Tennyson found his master-key. He held that the wish
to live, the desire for immortality, springs

> "from what we have
> The likest God within the soul";

and this seemed to the poet good presumptive evidence of
the fact of immortality. "If," he once said, "you allow
a God and God allows this strong instinct and universal
yearning for another life, surely that is in a measure a
presumption of its truth—we cannot give up the mighty
hopes that make us men."

To Bishop Lightfoot, on one occasion, he remarked that
"the cardinal point of Christianity is the life after death";
certainly this is true of Tennyson's own Christianity. Like
Browning, he believes that death could not dissolve human
personality. "I can hardly understand" (to quote the
poet's conversation once more) "how any great imaginative man who has deeply loved, suffered, thought, and
wrought, can doubt of the soul's continuous progress in
the after-life." Tennyson is specially the poet of immortality and the "intimations of immortality" are ever
with him. This was his master-thought; and no word

could sum up more accurately Tennyson's thought of Jesus than Paul's, when he said that Jesus "had brought life and incorruption to light through the gospel."

Seventh Week, Third Day

Of a truth I perceive that God is no respecter of persons: but in every nation he that feareth him, and worketh righteousness, is acceptable to him. The word which he sent unto the children of Israel, preaching good tidings of peace by Jesus Christ (he is Lord of all)—that saying ye yourselves know, which was published throughout all Judæa, beginning from Galilee, after the baptism which John preached; even Jesus of Nazareth, how that God anointed him with the Holy Ghost and with power: who went about doing good, and healing all that were oppressed of the devil; for God was with him.—Acts 10: 34-38.

We have seen that Browning found his clue to the tangle of thought in the story of Jesus. He held that in the Gospel man finds

> "A new truth; no conviction gains
> Of an old one only, made intense
> By a fresh appeal to his faded sense."

But Tennyson found his clue in himself, in his own intuitions; and what Jesus appeared to have done was to bring out into the sunlight things that were already in men's hearts. Jesus, says Browning, brought a new thing into the world; according to Tennyson, He called out and interpreted existing things in human nature. These things were indeed only dimly felt and dimly understood, but they were there all the time.

> "Though truths in manhood darkly join
> Deep-seated in our mystic frame,
> We yield all blessing to the name
> Of Him that made them current coin;

For Wisdom dealt with mortal powers
　　Where truth in closest words shall fail,
　　When truth embodied in a tale
Shall enter in at lowly doors.

And so the Word had breath and wrought
　　With human hands the creed of creeds
　　In loveliness of perfect deeds,
More strong than all poetic thought;

Which he may read that binds the sheaf
　　Or builds the house, or digs the grave,
　　And those wild eyes that watch the wave
In roarings round the coral reef."

"Truth embodied in a tale" is, of course, the gospel story of Jesus, "the revelation of the eternal thought of the universe." And since God reveals Himself to man and man is dimly aware of the revelation, it follows that the Word that had breath will bring to light and interpret all those intuitions which, according to Tennyson, represent the things that God communicates to our souls. We are to find our deepest aspirations and longings perfectly exposed and expounded in the Incarnate Word, not, mark, in His teaching, but in His life, His character, His work; for "the creed of creeds" was wrought out "in loveliness of perfect deeds." What Jesus does is to interpret us to ourselves. He, by His own life, brings "life and incorruption to light."

Seventh Week, Fourth Day

And Jesus cried and said, He that believeth on me, believeth not on me, but on him that sent me. And he that beholdeth me beholdeth him that sent me. I am come a light into the world, that whosoever believeth on me may not abide in the darkness. And if any man hear my sayings, and keep them not, I judge him not: for I came not to judge the world, but to save the world. He that rejecteth me, and receiveth not my sayings, hath one

that judgeth him: the word that I spake, the same shall
judge him in the last day. For I spake not from myself;
but the Father which sent me, he hath given me a commandment, what I should say, and what I should speak.
And I know that his commandment is life eternal: the
things therefore which I speak, even as the Father hath
said unto me, so I speak.—John 12: 44-50.

Tennyson constantly refused to commit himself to any
formal definition of the person of Christ; but it is quite
clear that no view of Him would have seemed adequate
to Tennyson which regarded Him only as a unique human
figure. To our poet, Jesus was the incarnate Word, whatever content so amazing a description might possess.
Tennyson probably felt that the whole significance of
Christ, even if it could be apprehended by the mind, was
not to be stated in a form of words. More great and
staggering things have been said about Jesus than of any
other person in history; and men still go on saying such
things. It would appear as though we had been twenty
centuries trying to capture the whole meaning of Jesus;
it still eludes us. It is just what has not yet been said
about Jesus that constitutes His real distinctiveness.

Tennyson, it is clear, felt the vast fascination of the
person of Jesus and stood with unshod feet in His presence. "I am always amazed," he says, "when I read the
New Testament at the splendour of Christ's purity and
holiness, and at His infinite pity." And it was the person of Jesus that Tennyson found at the heart of the
Gospel—not His teachings, nor the kind of philosophy
that might be built up around them. There is a refine-
ment of faith which seeks to escape the critical difficulties
of the gospel records by exalting the spirit of Jesus at
the expense of the historical figure, by magnifying what
He stood for at the expense of His person—as though
one could ever guess "what He stood for" without being
fairly sure of what He was. This distinction Tennyson
perceived to be entirely futile. "Christianity with its

divine morality, but without the central figure of Christ, the Son of Man, would become cold."

Seventh Week, Fifth Day

Blessed be the God and Father of our Lord Jesus Christ, who hath blessed us with every spiritual blessing in the heavenly places in Christ: even as he chose us in him before the foundation of the world, that we should be holy and without blemish before him in love: having foreordained us unto adoption as sons through Jesus Christ unto himself, according to the good pleasure of his will, to the praise of the glory of his grace, which he freely bestowed on us in the Beloved: in whom we have our redemption through his blood, the forgiveness of our trespasses, according to the riches of his grace, which he made to abound toward us in all wisdom and prudence, having made known unto us the mystery of his will, according to his good pleasure which he purposed in him unto a dispensation of the fulness of the times, to sum up all things in Christ, the things in the heavens, and the things upon the earth; in him, I say, in whom also we were made a heritage, having been foreordained according to the purpose of him who worketh all things after the counsel of his will; to the end that we should be unto the praise of his glory, we who had before hoped in Christ: in whom ye also, having heard the word of the truth, the gospel of your salvation,—in whom, having also believed, ye were sealed with the Holy Spirit of promise, which is an earnest of our inheritance, unto the redemption of God's own possession, unto the praise of his glory.—Eph. 1: 3-14.

In "Saul" Browning makes David argue that love, whether in men or in God, is of the same kind and would do the same thing—so that the revelation of the divine love in Jesus was not in a precise sense the "new truth" that Browning elsewhere said it was. But it is in Tennyson that we find the most complete expression of the feeling that the revelation of divine love in Jesus was also the perfect revelation of human love. This is seen in the way in which Tennyson dwells upon the name "Son of Man"; and it is the ground of an optimism which he shared with his great contemporary.

And to Tennyson as to Browning, though not with the same entire certainty, this thought of the perfect love revealed in Jesus brought genuine relief from the harshness of the new revelations of science. The thought of love as underlying the movement of the world might not explain why there can be no progress without suffering, but it helps us to be patient and hopeful in the faith that the end of everything must be good. It is, indeed, only such a confidence that can keep us in peace amid the contradictions and brokenness of nature and of our own life. Such a confidence, however, requires a great act of faith, which even more to Tennyson than to us seemed unwarranted in the face of scientific knowledge. And with a lingering disquiet in his mind, which never quite forsook him, Tennyson made this act of faith; and the love he believed to be the ground of all things helped him to overcome the unrest and doubt evoked by the tale of science, the witness of history, and the common experience of life, and to look calmly out upon the future. His optimism was not perhaps so robust as Browning's, yet his sense that the world is moving onward to some glorious goal was very deep and eager. In "Locksley Hall" he had sung,

"Yet I doubt not through the ages one increasing purpose runs";

and in the sequel, "Sixty Years After," he foretells the time on earth, when

"Every tiger madness muzzled, every serpent passion killed,
  Every grim ravine a garden, every blazing desert tilled,

Robed in universal harvest up to either pole she smiles,
  Universal ocean softly washing all her warless Isles";

and then, away beyond the frontiers of time, he sees the final end of all in God:

117

> "That God, which ever lives and loves,
>   One God, one law, one element,
>   And one far-off divine event
> To which the whole creation moves."

Seventh Week, Sixth Day

In the beginning was the Word, and the Word was with God, and the Word was God. The same was in the beginning with God. All things were made by him; and without him was not anything made that hath been made. In him was life; and the life was the light of men. And the light shineth in the darkness; and the darkness apprehended it not. There came a man, sent from God, whose name was John. The same came for witness, that he might bear witness of the light, that all might believe through him. He was not the light, but came that he might bear witness of the light. There was the true light, even the light which lighteth every man, coming into the world. He was in the world, and the world was made by him, and the world knew him not. He came unto his own, and they that were his own received him not. But as many as received him, to them gave he the right to become children of God, even to them that believe on his name: which were born, not of blood, nor of the will of the flesh, nor of the will of man, but of God. And the Word became flesh, and dwelt among us (and we beheld his glory, glory as of the only begotten from the Father), full of grace and truth.—John 1: 1-14.

Tennyson said that when he used the word *love* concerning God, he used it in the same sense as that of the Fourth Gospel. And if we are right in saying that Tennyson's view of Jesus' mission is described by St. Paul's phrase, "He brought life and incorruption to light through the gospel," we may also say that his view of the *person* of Jesus was identical with that of the Fourth Gospel.

He calls Jesus "Strong Son of God" in the prologue to "In Memoriam"; and it is interesting to recall that he once said that "the Son of Man is the most tremendous title possible." Son of God, Son of Man—so Jesus was to Tennyson. He did not attempt to distinguish between the humanity and the divinity of Jesus, and turn Him, as so many theologians have unwittingly done, into a sort of mythological demi-god. To Tennyson Jesus was all human, all divine—

> "Thou seemest human and divine,
>   The highest, holiest manhood, thou";

that is to say, one of ourselves, a man like one of us; and yet so high above us that we fall down before Him—

> "Our wills are ours, we know not how;
>   Our wills are ours, to make them thine."

All that the Fourth Gospel attributes to the Word, Tennyson ascribes to Jesus Christ. "All things were made by Him," says the ancient writer, and the modern poet puts it in this way:

> "Thine are these orbs of light and shade,
>   Thou madest Life in man and brute";

the former goes on: "In him was life; and the life was the light of men." Tennyson follows:

> "Thou madest Death, and lo! thy foot
> Is on the skull which thou hast made."

> "Thou wilt not leave us in the dust:
>   Thou madest man, he knows not why,
>   He thinks he was not made to die,
> And Thou hast made him; Thou art just."

"There was the true light which lighteth every man coming into the world," wrote the evangelist; and our poet says the same thing in his own way:

> "Our little systems have their day,
>   They have their day, and cease to be;
>   They are but broken lights of Thee,
> And Thou, O Lord, art more than they."

Seventh Week, Seventh Day

But now hath Christ been raised from the dead, the
firstfruits of them that are asleep. For since by man
came death, by man came also the resurrection of the
dead. For as in Adam all die, so also in Christ shall all
be made alive. But each in his own order: Christ the
firstfruits; then they that are Christ's, at his coming.
Then cometh the end, when he shall deliver up the kingdom to God, even the Father; when he shall have abolished all rule and all authority and power. For he must
reign, till he hath put all his enemies under his feet. The
last enemy that shall be abolished is death. For, He put
all things in subjection under his feet. But when he
saith, All things are put in subjection, it is evident that
he is excepted who did subject all things unto him. And
when all things have been subjected unto him, then shall
the Son also himself be subjected to him that did subject all things unto him, that God may be all in all.—
I Cor. 15: 20-28.

"Who knows," Tennyson once asked, "whether Revelation be not itself a veil to hide the glory of that love
which we could not look upon without marring our sight
and our onward progress?" In the presence of "these
unfathomable mysteries," humility and reverence are alone
becoming. The bigotry of the man who believes that his
formulæ contain all the faith, and who curses those who
question them, and the boastings of the man who loudly
vaunts his emancipation from the forms of faith, are
alike the symptoms of a dangerous pride wholly inconsistent with advancement into real light. Tennyson sym-
pathized with those who held that formal statements of
the truth cannot contain all the truth; and he felt that

> "There lives more faith in honest doubt,
> Believe me, than in half the creeds."

Yet it is expedient that faith should be cast into forms
and statements, and no harm is done so long as these
forms are only provisional and temporary and it is recognized that they are subject to change and modification as

"knowledge grows from more to more." The essence of faith can never change; that must remain constant through all the changes that may come to the forms in which successive ages have cast it, until it at length emerges free and glorious, untainted by the passions of men, unlimited by their narrowness—that truth which came by Jesus Christ. As the spirit of faith grows, so will the soul of goodness grow, until the spirit of Jesus, in religion, in conduct, in the whole of life, personal and social, shall be enthroned for evermore. And it is the strong, eager yearning for this glad time that he expresses in perhaps the best known of all his lines:

> "Ring out false pride in place and blood,
>   The civic slander and the spite;
>   Ring in the love of truth and right,
> Ring in the common love of good.
>
> Ring out old shapes of foul disease.
>   Ring out the narrowing lust of gold;
>   Ring out the thousand wars of old,
> Ring in the thousand years of peace.
>
> Ring in the valiant man and free,
>   The larger heart, the kindlier hand,
>   Ring out the darkness of the land,
> Ring in the Christ that is to be."

But while yet the vision of the future seemed afar off, the poet put his trust in Christ for the immediate business of life and death. In his own words concerning Mary the sister of Lazarus, his gaze rested on "the Life indeed." And so he was sustained in life; and as he passed, he was able to say:

> "For though from out our bourne of Time and Place
>   The flood may bear me far,
> I hope to see my Pilot face to face
>   When I have crossed the bar."

SUGGESTIONS FOR THOUGHT AND DISCUSSION

1. What is it in the story of Jesus that casts most light upon the problem of immortality?

2. Can you suggest any reason why Tennyson appears to take comparatively little notice of the death of Jesus?

3. *"Believing where we cannot prove."* How does belief differ from knowledge? Distinguish between a belief and an opinion.

4. What do you think Tennyson meant by "the Christ that is to be"?

CHAPTER VIII

The Poet as Mystic—Francis Thompson

(1859—1907)

The story of Francis Thompson is one of those true romances which are stranger than fiction. He was a Lancashire lad; and the rest of the external aspects of his life can be summed up in a few sentences. Too shy and feckless to make a priest—he had been born a Roman Catholic—he tried for a time to study medicine at Manchester and gave it up because his heart was not in it. Then he went in for a soldier and was refused because he had no physique. After that he went to London to try his luck, became an assistant in a boot and shoe shop, and afterwards a bookseller's messenger, and was a dead failure at both. Then he became a seller of newspapers and a caller of cabs. At this point, by what might seem a happy chance but was in reality a providential disposition, his genius was discovered and he fell into the hands of good friends, Wilfrid and Alice Meynell, who cherished him, and so far as his incurable eccentricity would permit, looked after him. Though he died at forty-eight—nineteen years after the Meynells had taken him to their hearts—he lived to write poetry which stands worthily in the company of immortal song. The story of his early struggles is one of singular pathos, and should be read in Everard Meynell's "Life of Francis Thompson." Door after door, not only of usefulness but of bare subsistence, shut in his face with a sort of brutal finality; and though he had weaknesses he might have overcome and habits he need never have contracted, one's pity for him never fails. He was cursed with a certain obstinate futility in affairs, a fact to some extent explained by the discovery that never more than a small part of the man dwelt in the concrete brick and mortar world. It was his happy lot, even amid his physical misery, to live and move among the stars. And looking at his life as a whole, pity becomes an impertinence. There is room only for wonderment and thankfulness. For out of the sweat and tears and privations of London streets, he drew the materials, if not the inspiration, of deathless song.

His music is that of a soul which dragged the weariest depths of life and drank the last and bitterest dregs of its cup. There is blood and anguish and iron in it; though the song itself is in the heavens, it never loses the clinging undertone of the depths. This was a man drawn to the last edge of life, walking, as it were, helplessly upon the utmost precipice; but his extremity became his university; and the lore of that hard school is the richest knowledge of mortal man. God sent Francis Thompson to tramp the Strand in weariness and dereliction, that he might tell the world how one may see

> "the traffic of Jacob's ladder
> Pitched between heaven and Charing Cross;

He sent him to wander forlornly on the Embankment through long, forsaken nights, that he might sing to a gross and clay-minded world a song of

> "Christ walking on the waters
> Not of Gennesaret but Thames."

And at a later time, when he came to survey the hard and desperate road he had traveled, he saw that he had not been the sport of an ironic fate but a fugitive from the divine love. It is this acknowledgment that throughout his life—had he but known it—he had been pursued by a love that would not let him go that he has sung in that imperishable ode called "The Hound of Heaven." The poem is not a fabric of arbitrary or groundless fancy, a pious fiction. It is the transcript of a living experience, the story of the lost sheep which the Shepherd went forth into the wilderness to seek, and sought until He found it.

We call Thompson a mystic; but the word mystic covers many things. Here the word is used simply to describe one who is familiar with the unseen world, finds in everything that is a gate which opens on the invisible, and knows his way about the world of spiritual reality. To such a man the things that are unseen and eternal are the supreme realities, his meat and his drink; and it is of such things that Francis Thompson sings. This, however, must not be taken to mean that the poet was incapable of reasoned judgment upon men and things. His prose is full of profound and penetrating reflection—as it is also of unusual richness of style. His essay on Shelley was hailed as a literary event of the first importance when it appeared in the *Dublin Review*. Incidentally, it should be said that Thompson's essay on Shelley is also an extraordinary piece of self-revelation—as indeed, all good criticism should be.

[Francis Thompson's work in poetry and prose is published in three large volumes, edited by Wilfrid Meynell. There is, however, a small and convenient volume available, "The Selected Poems of Francis Thompson."]

DAILY READINGS

Eighth Week, First Day

In that hour came the disciples unto Jesus, saying, Who then is greatest in the kingdom of heaven? And he called to him a little child, and set him in the midst of them, and said, Verily I say unto you, Except ye turn, and become as little children, ye shall in no wise enter into the kingdom of heaven. Whosoever therefore shall humble himself as this little child, the same is the greatest in the kingdom of heaven. And whoso shall receive one such little child in my name receiveth me: but whoso shall cause one of these little ones which believe on me to stumble, it is profitable for him that a great millstone should be hanged about his neck, and that he should be sunk in the depth of the sea.—Matt. 18: 1-6.

The first thing to be said about Francis Thompson is that he had the heart of a child; he had it and never lost it. In his essay on Shelley, he says: "Know you what it is to be a child? It is to be something very different from the man of today. It is to have a spirit yet streaming from the waters of baptism; it is to believe in love, to believe in loveliness, to believe in belief; it is to be so little that the elves can reach to whisper in your ear; it is to turn pumpkins into coaches and mice into horses, and nothing into everything; for each child has its fairy godmother in its own soul; it is to live in a nutshell and to count yourself the king of infinite space; it is

> 'To see a world in a grain of sand
>   And heaven in a wild flower
> Hold infinity in the palm of your hand
>   And eternity in an hour.' "

And in this passage, he was describing his own mind. Most men as they grow older lose the sensitiveness, the faith, the wonder of the child mind, and in their folly deem that they have become wise—forgetting how great things "are revealed unto babes." But Francis Thompson never lost this essential childlikeness and it is the clue to his own soul. It was because he remained in heart "a little child" that he saw so plainly the kingdom of God.

His poems about and to children are in consequence full of genuine and unchanging charm. Perhaps the greatest experience in his life was his admission to the heart of the Meynell family, and it is to the children of that home that most of his child-poems are addressed.

Probably he felt more at home in the company of children than anywhere else; and in the poem which he wrote to his godson, Francis Meynell, he gives us an example of the quaint humor which must have endeared him to all children:

"And when, immortal mortal, droops your head,
    And you, the child of deathless song, are dead;
    Then as you search with unaccustomed glance
    The ranks of Paradise for my countenance
    Turn not your tread along the Uranian[1] sod
    Among the bearded counsellors of God;
    For if in Eden as on earth are we,
    I sure shall keep a younger company. . . .
    Look for me in the nurseries of Heaven."

But this is, of course, much more than mere quaintness. It is the essential subsoil of Thompson's mind; and it is always natural for him to sing in this way:

"Little Jesus, wast Thou shy
        Once, and just so small as I?
        And what did it feel like to be
        Out of Heaven and just like me? . . .
        Thou canst not have forgotten all
        That it feels like to be small:
        And Thou know'st I cannot pray
        To Thee in my father's way—
        When Thou wast so little, say,
        Couldst Thou talk Thy Father's way?—
        So, a little Child, come down
        And hear a child's tongue like Thy own;
        Take me by the hand and walk
        And listen to my baby talk.
        To Thy Father show my prayer
        (He will look, Thou art so fair,)
        And say: 'O Father, I, Thy Son,
        Bring the prayer of a little one.'
        And He will smile, that children's tongue
        Has not changed since Thou wast young."

---

[1] *Uranian,* a word our poet frequently uses, simply means celestial.

Eighth Week, Second Day

And Paul stood in the midst of the Areopagus, and said,

Ye men of Athens, in all things I perceive that ye are somewhat superstitious. For as I passed along, and observed the objects of your worship, I found also an altar with this inscription, To An Unknown God. What therefore ye worship in ignorance, this set I forth unto you. The God that made the world and all things therein, he, being Lord of heaven and earth, dwelleth not in temples made with hands; neither is he served by men's hands, as though he needed anything, seeing he himself giveth to all life, and breath, and all things; and he made of one every nation of men for to dwell on all the face of the earth, having determined their appointed seasons, and the bounds of their habitation; that they should seek God, if haply they might feel after him, and find him, though he is not far from each one of us: for in him we live, and move, and have our being; as certain even of your own poets have said, For we are also his offspring. Being then the offspring of God, we ought not to think that the Godhead is like unto gold, or silver, or stone, graven by art and device of man. The times of ignorance therefore God overlooked; but now he commandeth men that they should all everywhere repent: inasmuch as he hath appointed a day, in the which he will judge the world in righteousness by the man whom he hath ordained; whereof he hath given assurance unto all men, in that he hath raised him from the dead.—Acts 17: 22-31.

Thompson, having the heart of a child, was very sensitive to symbols; and the rich and varied symbolism of the Catholic Church provided him with endless suggestion and imagery. For instance, he begins his "Orient Ode" in this way:

> "Lo, in the sanctuaried East
> Day, a dedicated priest
> In all his robes pontifical exprest,
> Lifteth slowly, lifteth sweetly
> From out its Orient tabernacle drawn."

And this kind of language is characteristic of his verse. But it must not be supposed that it was only imagery. It was in a very real sense also interpretation; and it raises a question of some importance for Protestants. In their revolt from Rome our forefathers left almost all symbolism behind them and came to worship God in what Father Tyrrell has called "circumstances of sought-out plainness." This was indeed natural, seeing that superstition had gathered around the rites of the Church. Yet the fact remains that symbolism has its uses. During the last few years we have exalted the symbols of patriotism, we salute the Stars and Stripes or the Union Jack; we have even introduced them into our churches. But our churches are almost invariably bare of the characteristic symbols of Christianity. That may be right or wrong; but it is a question worth thinking about. There are few people who do not find a symbol an aid to the focusing of attention; the symbol might serve also as an aid to religious devotion. Provided the obvious dangers of symbolism are recognized and guarded against, there is something to be said for their restoration to our religious practice.

But what is chiefly interesting here is that the great central symbol of Catholicism, the sacrifice of the mass, became to Francis Thompson a clue to the universe. The mass, because he believed it to be the continuation of the sacrifice of the Cross, seems to give to everything a redemptive significance. "Thou," he says to the setting sun,

> "Thou dost image, thou dost follow
>   That King-maker of Creation
>   Who, ere Hellas hailed Apollo
>   Gave thee, angel-god, thy station.
> Thou art of Him a type memorial:
> Like Him thou hangest in dreadful pomp of blood
>   Upon thy Western rood,
> And His stained brow did veil like thine tonight,
>   Yet lift once more Its light."

To Thompson, all nature was sacramental, full of intimations of divinity; and nature is perhaps too little suggestive of the redeeming grace of God to us because our sacraments have lost much of their significance for us. For after all, all the work of God must be of a piece; and as a modern mystic has said, "The Cross is the ground plan of the Universe." Francis Thompson's friend, Mrs. Meynell, has put the same thought at another angle in a little poem called "The Fugitive," evoked by the saying of a French publicist, *"Nous avons chassé ce Jésus-Christ,"* "We have driven out this Jesus Christ."

> "Yes, from the ingrate heart, the street
>   Of garrulous tongue, the warm retreat
>   Within the village and the town;
>   Not from the lands where ripen brown
> A thousand thousand hills of wheat;
>
> Not from the long Burgundian line
> The southward, sunward range of vine.
>   Hunted, He never will escape
>   The flesh, the blood, the sheaf, the grape,
> That feed His man—the bread, the wine."

When we allow for the Catholic presuppositions of the poet, what remains is this—that "His secret presence in creation's veins" is universal, and more, it is redemptive in all its reactions. This is the Immanent Christ, who cannot be driven from His world, who is in and through everything that is in it in order that He may redeem it, and this is peculiarly the Christ of Francis Thompson.

Eighth Week, Third Day

O Lord, thou hast searched me, and known me.
Thou knowest my downsitting and mine uprising,
Thou understandest my thought afar off.
Thou searchest out my path and my lying down,
And art acquainted with all my ways.
For there is not a word in my tongue,
But, lo, O Lord, thou knowest it altogether.

Thou hast beset me behind and before,
And laid thine hand upon me.
Such knowledge is too wonderful for me;
It is high, I cannot attain unto it.
Whither shall I go from thy spirit?
Or whither shall I flee from thy presence?
If I ascend up into heaven, thou art there:
If I make my bed in Sheol, behold, thou art there.
If I take the wings of the morning,
And dwell in the uttermost parts of the sea;
Even there shall thy hand lead me,
And thy right hand shall hold me.
If I say, Surely the darkness shall overwhelm me,
And the light about me shall be night;
Even the darkness hideth not from thee,
But the night shineth as the day:
The darkness and the light are both alike to thee.
—Psalm 139: 1-12.

It is probable that Francis Thompson will be best known by "The Hound of Heaven." It is one of those utterances which, by their authentic and self-verifying note of reality, fix the meaning and the truth of the eternal Gospel in men's minds forever. That which can be so sung must be everlastingly real and true. Fictions and illusions evoke no such mighty music. There is a poetry of the imagination which has its own peculiar immortality; its subject matter and end is beauty; its reaction is purely emotional and esthetic. But there is also a poetry of experience; and its theme is life, reality, the deep things of God; and its reaction is to change men's lives. The one pleases—even to the point of ecstasy; the other sweeps you off your feet or cuts down to the marrow of your soul; and once you have heard its great searching tones, you can never be quite the same man any more. This is the class to which "The Hound of Heaven" belongs. Not that it lacks beauty; it is extraordinarily beautiful. But here beauty was Thompson's handmaid rather than his mistress. His great personal discovery was the mysterious, relentless love of God; and in "The Hound of Heaven," it is this deepest thing of God that he has sung in undying song. He has set the ultimate word of God to the rarest human music.

In dull prose the argument of the poem is this: The spirit of man is beset by an insatiable hunger; and it is dimly aware of a satisfaction adequate to the hunger. But it is also aware that this supreme satisfaction is unavailable except at the price of a full self-surrender. But the soul shrinks from this surrender, because it fears that it entails the loss of all the joyous and beautiful things of the world. Unwilling to pay this price of perfect satisfaction, it turns to seek it in those fair things that are nearer and less exacting—in human love, in the spacious wonder of the universe, in the innocent company of little children, in intimate communion with nature. All these give promise, but deny the substance of satisfaction and fail the spirit in its sore need. At last the soul gives up the search in despair, and all it has to show for its long quest is a wasted, charred, broken life. Yet all this time its patient Pursuer has been at its heels; and now at last the shattered and disillusioned soul waits helplessly for the coming of this unyielding and inevasible "hound." In its extremity, the Pursuer finds it, and the chase is over. The spirit surrenders to its captor, and in its capture finds the fulness it longed for in the everlasting mercy from which it was so long a fugitive.

Eighth Week, Fourth Day

O Lord, our Lord,
How excellent is thy name in all the earth!
Who hast set thy glory upon the heavens.
Out of the mouth of babes and sucklings hast thou established strength,
Because of thine adversaries,
That thou mightest still the enemy and the avenger.
When I consider thy heavens, the work of thy fingers,
The moon and the stars, which thou hast ordained;
What is man, that thou art mindful of him?
And the son of man, that thou visitest him?

For thou hast made him but little lower than God,
And crownest him with glory and honour.
Thou madest him to have dominion over the works of
    thy hands;
Thou hast put all things under his feet:
All sheep and oxen,
Yea, and the beasts of the field;
The fowl of the air, and the fish of the sea,
Whatsoever passeth through the paths of the seas.
O Lord, our Lord,
How excellent is thy name in all the earth!
                                                —Psalm 8.

When the poet tells of his failure to find self-fulfilment in human love, we are reminded of how a greater than he, Dante, cheated of the love of Beatrice Portinari, set out to sing a more wondrous love. It was a thwarted love that gave the world "The Divine Comedy," because it threw Dante back on his search for God; but it is the vanity of human love for the ultimate human need that drives the fugitive of our poem away from it. And when he tells us how he sought peace

> "across the margent of the world . . .
> And troubled the gold gateways of the stars,"

we recall what Kant once said, that, next to the moral consciousness of man, the thing that moved him most was the starry firmament of heaven. Here our poet treads ancient and obvious ground. From the beginning man has looked in the eyes of man and in the face of heaven for the word and the bread of life—yet ever in vain. Thompson strikes a new note when he tells how he sought the joy he lacked in the innocence of little children:

> "I sought no more that, after which I strayed
>   In face of man or maid;
> But still within the little children's eyes
>   Seems something, something that replies,
> *They* at least are for me, surely for me!"

133

And indeed here the poet was not far from the Kingdom
of God—not far, yet

> "Just as their young eyes grew sudden fair
>   With dawning answers there,
>   Their angel plucked them from me by the hair."

Denied by the children, he turns to nature. He

> "Drew the bolt of Nature's secrecies.
>   I knew all the swift importings
>   On the wilful face of skies;
>   I knew how the clouds arise
>   Spumed of the wild sea-snortings;
>   All that's born or dies,
>   Rose and drooped with—made them shapers
> Of mine own moods, or wailful or divine."

Yet nature proves like the rest a broken reed.

"But not by that, by that was eased my human smart,
In vain my tears were wet on Heaven's grey cheek,
For ah, we know not what each other says,
    These things and I; in sound *I* speak,
Their sound is but their stir; they speak by silences.
Nature, poor stepdame, cannot slake my drouth; . . .
Never did any milk of hers once bless
    My thirsting mouth."

He had knocked at every door; and none had opened to
let him in.

Eighth Week, Fifth Day

And he spake unto them this parable, saying, What
man of you, having a hundred sheep, and having lost one
of them, doth not leave the ninety and nine in the wilderness, and go after that which is lost, until he find it?
And when he hath found it, he layeth it on his shoulders,
rejoicing. And when he cometh home, he calleth together
his friends and his neighbours, saying unto them, Rejoice
with me, for I have found my sheep which was lost. I
say unto you, that even so there shall be joy in heaven

over one sinner that repenteth, more than over ninety
and nine righteous persons, which need no repentance.
—Luke 15: 3-7.

After nature fails him, the fugitive gives up the quest.
In his frustration and despair he reviews his life.

> "In the rash lustihood of my young powers
> I shook the pillaring hours
> And pulled my life upon me; grimed with smears
> I stand amid the dust of the mounded years—
> My mangled youth lies dead beneath the heap,
> My days have crackled and gone up in smoke,
> Have puffed and burnt as sun-starts on a stream."

This is all he has to show for all his feverish quest—the
smoking ruins of his life. He wonders what is yet to
come; and looking into the mists of the future, he sees
no goal or end but the darkness of death.

It is to be observed that this is the story of a soul
which sought the ends of life along paths in themselves
fair and lovely. It is not the story of the *roué* or the
sensualist. John Masefield, in his poem "The Everlasting
Mercy," has transcribed the theme of "The Hound of
Heaven" to the key of low life. There the Hound pursues
its quarry through the gutter and the mire; but Francis
Thompson is singing of a soul that had not willingly been
stained with vice and had not haunted the gaily-lit highways of gross sin. He had turned to fill the unfilled
spaces of his soul with love and beauty; but he came away
from the altars where he had worshiped empty-handed.
For whatever he found there, he knew he had not found
the one thing needful. It is just that insatiable hunger
still unsatisfied, that unredeemed misery which Francis
Thompson has put into poignant verse in the first part of
the poem.

The last stanza of the poem tells of the capture and the
surrender. The spirit hears the footfall of the Pursuer;
the Hound has found its quarry.

"That Voice is round me like a bursting sea:
   'And is thy earth so marred,
     Shattered in shard on shard?
Lo, all things fly thee, for thou fliest Me.' . . .

All which I took from thee, I did but take
   Not for thy harms,
But just that thou might'st seek it in My arms.
   All which thy child's mistake
Fancies as lost, I have stored for thee at home;
     Rise, clasp My hand, and come."

"He goeth forth into the wilderness . . . *until he find it.*"
And so this troubled soul was found at last.

Eighth Week, Sixth Day

At that season Jesus answered and said, I thank thee,
O Father, Lord of heaven and earth, that thou didst hide
these things from the wise and understanding, and didst
reveal them unto babes: yea, Father, for so it was well-
pleasing in thy sight. All things have been delivered
unto me of my Father: and no one knoweth the Son, save
the Father; neither doth any know the Father, save the
Son, and he to whomsoever the Son willeth to reveal him.
Come unto me, all ye that labour and are heavy laden,
and I will give you rest. Take my yoke upon you,
and learn of me; for I am meek and lowly in heart: and
ye shall find rest unto your souls. For my yoke is easy,
and my burden is light.—Matt. 11: 25-30.

"Thou madest us for Thyself," said Augustine, "and
our heart is never at rest until it rest in Thee." But more
than this is true—God is forever seeking to bring us to
Himself, that we may have rest in His love. And this
is the moral of "The Hound of Heaven":

"Halts by me that footfall:
   Is my gloom, after all,
Shade of His hand, outstretched caressingly?
   'Ah, fondest, blindest, weakest,
   I am He whom thou seekest!
Thou dravest love from thee, who dravest Me.'"

The lineaments of this "tremendous Lover" are plain to see; and it is Francis Thompson's gift to us that he enables us to realize that the Incarnation is the great symbol of God's search for us. We bid men seek God; and it is right and needful so to do; but that is only one half of the truth. The other half is that God is forever seeking us. And we may even say that when men set out in search of God, God (as Pascal said long ago) has already *found* them. All through the poem, the fugitive is aware that the Pursuer is close on to him, coming

> "With unhurrying chase
> And unperturbéd pace,
> Deliberate speed, majestic instancy,"

and all the time sure of his quarry. It is that divine love "that will not let me go," and pursues me, into the desert of my self-sufficiency, in the wilderness of my sin, among the mountains of my ignorance—until He find me. And God sent His Son into the world to show us plainly what He is about, at what infinite cost He is pursuing us. His Son went out into the wilderness before our eyes, and

> "None of the ransomed ever knew
> How deep were the waters crossed,"

that He might bring us back to God. That, surely, is the heart and pith of the Good News.

There is no escape from this Lover. At least, Francis Thompson could not escape Him. He found Him at every turn. He says that everything in God's universe speaks of Christ.

> "When I with wingéd feet had run
> Through all the windy earth about,
> Quested its secret of the sun
> And heard what thing the stars together shout,"

it was this that he heard from every voice:

"By this, O singer, know we if thou see.
  When men shall say to thee: Lo, Christ is here;
  When men shall say to thee: Lo, Christ is there;
  Believe them: yea, and this—then art thou seer—
  When all thy crying clear
  Is but: Lo here, lo there! ah me, lo everywhere!"

"Ah me, lo everywhere!"   It is the Christ who is everywhere that Francis Thompson sees and sings.

Eighth Week, Seventh Day

And straightway he constrained the disciples to enter
into the boat, and to go before him unto the other side,
till he should send the multitudes away. And after he
had sent the multitudes away, he went up into the mountain apart to pray: and when even was come, he was
there alone. But the boat was now in the midst of the
sea, distressed by the waves; for the wind was contrary.
And in the fourth watch of the night he came unto them,
walking upon the sea. And when the disciples saw him
walking on the sea, they were troubled, saying, It is an
apparition; and they cried out for fear. But straightway
Jesus spake unto them, saying, Be of good cheer; it is
I; be not afraid.—Matt. 14: 22-27.

The omnipresent, ubiquitous Christ, to whom all things
bear witness, the immanent Christ whose glory breaks
through the crust of things upon those who have eyes to
see—this, then, is Francis Thompson's Christ.

We may recall that Dante found Christ in the midst of
the host of the redeemed in heaven; and we traced that
to the logic of medieval Catholicism. Yet even in that
day there were those who found Christ "closer than
breathing, nearer than hands or feet." In Thomas à
Kempis's "Imitation of Christ," we find an intimate, present Christ, and, while Francis Thompson is essentially
true to the Catholic tradition, he brings Christ down to
earth and finds Him always very near. It may be that
Thompson had ceased to think in purely spatial terms; it
would be natural for the mystic to find the veil between

heaven and earth so very thin that he would be hard put
to it to say where the one ended and the other began.
Thompson was very greatly influenced by William Blake;
and in Blake's prophecies it is very difficult sometimes to
say whether we are in the city of his dreams or in the
brick-and-mortar suburbs of London. His passage from
the one to the other is swift and bewildering. And in
Thompson's verse, heaven and earth jostle each other
with a strange intimacy.

> "O world invisible, we view thee
> O world intangible, we touch thee
> O world unknowable, we know thee
> Inapprehensible, we clutch thee! . . .
>
> Not where the wheeling systems darken,
> And our benumbed conceiving soars!—
> The drift of pinions, would we hearken,
> Beats at our own clay-shuttered doors.
>
> The angels keep their ancient places
> Turn but a stone and start a wing!
> 'Tis ye, 'tis your estrangéd faces
> That miss the many-splendoured thing.
>
> But when so sad, thou canst not sadder
> Cry; and upon thy so sore loss
> Shall shine the traffic of Jacob's ladder
> Pitched betwixt heaven and Charing Cross.
>
> Yea, in the night, my Soul, my daughter
> Cry—clinging Heaven by the hems
> And lo, Christ walking on the water
> Not of Gennesareth but Thames!"

*"Lo, I am with you alway, even unto the end of the
world."*

SUGGESTIONS FOR THOUGHT AND DISCUSSION

How would you describe the child mind? What did
Jesus mean by saying that except we turn and become as
little children we cannot enter into the Kingdom of God?

Some adverse criticism has been made of the title "The Hound of Heaven." Do you think this criticism justified in view of the theme of the poem?

Jesus once said that when men said of the Kingdom of Cod, "Lo, here" or "Lo, there," we were not to believe them. Is there any inconsistency between this and Francis Thompson's "Lo here, lo there, lo everywhere"?

CHAPTER IX

The Prophet of Righteousness— Savonarola

(1452—1498)

A hundred and eighty years after Dante had been exiled from Florence, there came thither a young Dominican monk whose name was destined to be associated with the city as intimately as Dante's own. Dante and Savonarola had much in common. Both possessed the deep historical insight and the passion for righteousness that marked the Hebrew prophets. Both plunged fearlessly into that vortex of intrigue and faction which constituted the political life of Florence, in the hope that they might deliver the city from the hands of greedy princes and their greedier friends. Both at length suffered the penalty of the prophet —exile for Dante, a martyr's death for Savonarola.

In the period between Dante and Savonarola much had happened, but the main characteristics had remained much the same. The same dissension and jealousy were tearing out the country's heart. The united Italy of which Dante had dreamed seemed no nearer; and indeed many centuries had yet to pass before the great Florentine's dream came true. As in Dante's time, so in Savonarola's, there was danger to Italy from the designs of French princes, though Savonarola and his contemporaries, reading history less deeply than their great precursor, were inclined at one time to hail the coming of a French King to Italy as a great deliverance. And the greatest trouble of all was

certainly the greed of the Papacy. The vicars of Christ
were conspicuous by their lack of the spirit of Christ; and
that great gulf which yawned between the temper of
Rome in Dante's day and the spirit of the Gospel had
become none the narrower at the end of the fifteenth
century. Dante's denunciations of the avarice and the
excesses of the Pope might have been repeated with equal
emphasis in the Italy of Savonarola.

The great happening of the period between Dante and
Savonarola was the rebirth of learning, commonly known
as the Renascence. It does not belong to our present
purpose to tell the story of the strange rediscovery of the
treasures of antiquity, with its profound effect upon
thought, literature, and art. The ancient world seemed
to be brought to life again. But in the clash of old with
new, there was of necessity much confusion of thought.
The impact of the philosophy of Greece upon the beliefs
of medieval Catholicism brought about an intellectual
twilight in which many strange things were said and done;
and it is full of interest to observe men in that day, as in
the case of Browning and Tennyson we saw men doing
the same thing in a later day, seeking to work out an
intelligible position between the old light and the new.

DAILY READINGS

Ninth Week, First Day

Woe to them that are at ease in Zion, and to them that
are secure in the mountain of Samaria, the notable men
of the chief of the nations, to whom the house of Israel
come! Pass ye unto Calneh, and see; and from thence
go ye to Hamath the great: then go down to Gath of the
Philistines: be they better than these kingdoms? or is
their border greater than your border? Ye that put
far away the evil day, and cause the seat of violence to
come near; that lie upon beds of ivory, and stretch themselves upon their couches, and eat the lambs out of the
flock, and the calves out of the midst of the stall; that

sing idle songs to the sound of the viol; that devise for themselves instruments of music, like David; that drink wine in bowls, and anoint themselves with the chief ointments; but they are not grieved for the affliction of Joseph.—Amos 6: 1-6.

It was, then, in the midst of political, ecclesiastical, and intellectual confusion that Savonarola came to Florence. The city was renowned for the zeal with which it had fostered the new knowledge. Under Lorenzo de' Medici, known as the Magnificent, literature and art had been greatly encouraged. Lorenzo himself was a very complex character. A sincere friend of the arts, his personal life was of no high order. His government of Florence was harsh and unscrupulous; he resorted to many questionable means to secure his authority and to increase his wealth.

Savonarola's early years in Florence coincided with the later years of Lorenzo's reign. The monk, with his stern uncompromising demand for purity of life, had scant respect for the evil-living prince and made little effort to disguise his feeling. Lorenzo in his turn disliked Savonarola exceedingly. After a time of quiet service in training novitiates at the convent of St. Mark, Savonarola's great preaching gift asserted itself, and before long his name was known throughout Italy. Feeling with something like agony the corruption in Church and State, he condemned it unsparingly in both places, and it took the people no long time to recognize that a prophet had arisen, to whom they listened gladly. Utterly fearless, altogether sure of his message, wielding a unique spiritual power, he soon became the most considerable figure in Florence.

One incident shows the stuff of which he was made. Lorenzo on his deathbed sent for Savonarola to give him absolution. Savonarola laid down as a condition of absolution that he should restore the liberties of Florence. Lorenzo refused and Savonarola went away, leaving the dying prince unabsolved.

Ninth Week, Second Day

Then went I up in the night by the brook, and viewed
the wall; and I turned back, and entered by the valley
gate, and so returned. And the rulers knew not whither
I went, or what I did; neither had I as yet told it to the
Jews, nor to the priests, nor to the nobles, nor to the
rulers, nor to the rest that did the work. Then said I
unto them, Ye see the evil case that we are in, how
Jerusalem lieth waste, and the gates thereof are burned
with fire: come and let us build up the wall of Jerusalem,
that we be no more a reproach. And I told them of the
hand of my God which was good upon me; as also of the
king's words that he had spoken unto me. And they
said, Let us rise up and build. So they strengthened
their hands for the good work.—Neh. 2: 15-18.

Piero, Lorenzo's son, succeeded him. Possessing none
of his father's good qualities, he had all his worst ones
in an aggravated form. He was a weak profligate, and
the new life then stirring in Florence made his rule impossible. Some intrigue with Charles VIII of France,
who was then invading Italy, was made the occasion for
deposing him. In the events which followed Savonarola
was virtually governor of Florence. The new government
which was established was devised and secured by him.
The people accepted his counsel unquestioningly. A great
reformation of morals and manners coincided with the
political revolution, and Florence seemed to be at length
emerging into a new, vigorous, corporate life, based upon
righteousness and justice.

Of the political side of Savonarola's work, this is not
the place to write. That is a matter for the expert in
political science. But it belongs to our present inquiry
to observe that Savonarola established the principle that
no stable political institutions could ever be reared except
upon a definitely moral foundation. All political problems
are at bottom moral problems, and no amount of statesmanship or management can avail to secure the stability
of a political structure which is not first of all solidly
laid on the rock of morality.

In the central lobby of the British Houses of Parliament, there is inlaid in the tiled floor a Latin inscription. It is the scripture, "Except the Lord build the house, they labour in vain who build it." That is a good word for statesmen and for all who have building operations of any kind on hand. It is the acknowledgment that the statesmanship which is not foursquare with the will of God is doomed to failure; and this was the first article of Savonarola's faith.

And it was plain to the great preacher that morality itself must rest upon religion. The place of the prophet in the community is to teach and to evoke that genuine religious devotion upon which all stable institutions must be founded. Savonarola entered into the tumult of politics only unwillingly, for he conceived his peculiar office to be that of quickening the spirit and conscience necessary to good government. The business of the Church is not primarily with political ways and means, but with the creation of a public conscience which will determine the methods and ends of government in accordance with moral principles.

Ninth Week, Third Day

The word of God came unto John the son of Zacharias in the wilderness. And he came into all the region round about Jordan, preaching the baptism of repentance unto remission of sins; as it is written in the book of the words of Isaiah the prophet,

> The voice of one crying in the wilderness,
> Make ye ready the way of the Lord,
> Make his paths straight.
> Every valley shall be filled,
> And every mountain and hill shall be brought low;
> And the crooked shall become straight,
> And the rough ways smooth;
> And all flesh shall see the salvation of God.

He said therefore to the multitudes that went out to be baptized of him, Ye offspring of vipers, who warned

**you to flee from the wrath to come? Bring forth there-
fore fruits worthy of repentance.—Luke 3: 2-8.**

The first word of a prophet's message is *Repent;* and
this was Savonarola's first word to the people of Florence.
He had all the prophet's freedom from the trammels of
convention and tradition; but the intellectual twilight of
his time made it impossible for him to establish himself
in a clear, self-consistent position of thought. At one
moment, for instance, he seemed to accept without question the authority of the Church as expressed through the
Pope. At another, he insisted with the passion of a Luther
on the absolute supremacy of the Scriptures; and he does
not appear to have been aware of any conflict between
the two positions. But a prophet is the last person in
the world from whom to expect a logical consistency.
The force of circumstances, however, led Savonarola, as
time went on, to ascribe less authority to the Pope and
to make his appeal more and more to the Scriptures.

But outside the region of doctrine, Savonarola showed
no uncertainty of thought. He knew what religion was
and what conduct should be; and his call to his fellow-
townsmen to repent was uttered in tones that carried their
own authority with them. It should, however, not be
thought that Savonarola's call to repentance was a denial
of the joy of life or, as has been the case with some
prophets of a mere austere turn, a disparagement of
beauty.

It has been sometimes held that the Italian Renascence
was a resurrection of paganism; and no doubt the discovery of the wisdom and beauty of Greek antiquity did
for a moment and to some extent tend to dim the riches
of the Gospel. It is, indeed, no wonder that it should
be so. The interpretation of the Gospel that then held
the field was the dry and formal theology of the School-
men; and it was bound to suffer from the impact upon
it of the rediscovery of the undying "glory that was

Greece." Art and Literature flourished greatly under the influence of the Greek spirit. It has been assumed that because Savonarola withstood the undoubted paganism of Lorenzo's reign, he was an enemy of the arts and a hindrance to the new spirit. So far from this being true, Savonarola was, perhaps unconsciously, one of the means by which the Renascence came to flow in Christian channels. In his own convent of St. Mark, he encouraged the fine arts; and Michael Angelo and Botticelli, to name only two of the great Renascence artists, derived their inspiration very largely from Savonarola.

Repentance to Savonarola meant a change of heart that brought, not a narrower life, but a life more abundant.

Ninth Week, Fourth Day

Now I Paul myself intreat you by the meekness and gentleness of Christ, I who in your presence am lowly among you, but being absent am of good courage toward you: yea, I beseech you, that I may not when present shew courage with the confidence wherewith I count to be bold against some, which count of us as if we walked according to the flesh. For though we walk in the flesh, we do not war according to the flesh (for the weapons of our warfare are not of the flesh, but mighty before God to the casting down of strong holds); casting down imaginations, and every high thing that is exalted against the knowledge of God, and bringing every thought into captivity to the obedience of Christ.—II Cor. 10: 1-5.

It was, however, only as Savonarola broke away from the accepted theology and teaching of medieval Catholicism that he was able to give to artists, and to the common people as well, that enlarged liberal spirit in which the glories of the ancient world and the grace of Jesus Christ were to find a common meeting-ground, and in which the true proportions of both would appear. The utter and absolute supremacy of Jesus Christ, everywhere, in philosophy, in art, in statesmanship—this was the body of

Savonarola's message, as the call to repentance was its beginning.

In theory, Savonarola's attitude to the Church was correct enough. The Church Militant on earth was the other self of the Church Triumphant in heaven; and as the head of the latter was Jesus Christ, so was the Pope the head of the former. "Wherefore," he says in a little tractate called "The Triumph of the Cross," "it is manifest that all the faithful should be united under the Pope as the supreme head of the Roman Church, the mother of all other churches, and that whosoever departs from the unity of the Roman Church departs from the Church."

But whatever Savonarola's theory may have been, in practice he considers that his own supreme head is not the Pope but Jesus Christ. It may have been that he regarded the Pope of his own day as a usurper who had no right to the office he held; but Savonarola clearly regarded his own commission as held directly from Christ. When the Pope excommunicated him, he said, "For me, it is enough not to be interdicted by Christ." So lightly did he hold the excommunication that he went on to say, "O my Lord, if I should seek to be absolved from this excommunication, let me be sent to hell."

So impossible is it to hold new wine in old wineskins.

Ninth Week, Fifth Day

What then shall we say to these things? If God is for us, who is against us? He that spared not his own Son, but delivered him up for us all, how shall he not also with him freely give us all things? Who shall lay anything to the charge of God's elect? It is God that justifieth; who is he that shall condemn? It is Christ Jesus that died, yea rather, that was raised from the dead, who is at the right hand of God, who also maketh intercession for us. Who shall separate us from the love of Christ? shall tribulation, or anguish, or persecution, or famine, or nakedness, or peril, or sword? Even as it is written,

For thy sake we are killed all the day long;
We were accounted as sheep for the slaughter.

Nay, in all these things we are more than conquerors through him that loved us. For I am persuaded, that neither death, nor life, nor angels, nor principalities, nor things present, nor things to come, nor powers, nor height, nor depth, nor any other creature, shall be able to separate us from the love of God, which is in Christ Jesus our Lord.—Rom. 8: 31-39.

We may fairly trace in Savonarola the foreshadowing of that coming revolt from papal authority and that growing consciousness of the true relation of the Church, whether in heaven or in earth, to its only Head, which led to the Protestant Reformation. This tendency is quite evident throughout Savonarola's teaching. The complex machinery of the Roman system for the spiritual development of its children, he views with increasing distrust and he insists that the increase of ceremonies means a decrease of real spirituality. "Wherefore," he says, "we are come to declare to the world that outward worship must give way to inward, and that ceremonies are naught save as a means of stirring the spirit." The essence of the Christian religion is the love of Christ, "that lively affection which inspires the faithful with the desire to bring his soul to unity, as it were, with that of Christ; and live the life of the Lord not by external imitation but by inward and divine inspiration." In this love is the power to raise man "from humanity to divinity" and to unite "the finite creature to the infinite Creator." This love is the keynote of Savonarola's preaching. "Take the example of Christ," he says, in one of his sermons, "who came to us as a little child, in all things like unto the sons of men, submitting to hunger and thirst, to heat and cold and discomfort. What hath urged Him to do this? He spoke now with just men, now with publicans and sinners, and He led a life that all men and all women, small and great, rich and poor, may imitate, all after their own way and according to their condition, and thus undoubtedly win their salvation. And what made Him live so poor and so marvellous a life? It was undoubtedly Love. Love bound Him to the pillar, led Him to the Cross, raised Him from the dead, and made Him ascend into heaven and thus accomplish the mysteries of our redemption."

Savonarola's sense of personal union with Jesus was so intimate that when the tide turned and a fickle people turned against him, he declared, "They may kill me as they please, but they will never tear Christ from my heart." When at last Florence did come to kill him, a priest asked him, "In what spirit dost thou face this martyrdom?" the monk answered, "The Lord hath suffered so much for me." And as they fixed the halter around his neck, he said, "Into thy hands, O Lord, I commend my spirit."

Ninth Week, Sixth Day

Now when they had passed through Amphipolis and Apollonia, they came to Thessalonica, where was a synagogue of the Jews: and Paul, as his custom was, went in unto them, and for three sabbath days reasoned with them from the scriptures, opening and alleging, that it behoved the Christ to suffer, and to rise again from the dead; and that this Jesus, whom, said he, I proclaim unto you, is the Christ. And some of them were persuaded, and consorted with Paul and Silas; and of the devout Greeks a great multitude, and of the chief women not a few. But the Jews, being moved with jealousy, took unto them certain vile fellows of the rabble, and gathering a crowd, set the city on an uproar; and assaulting the house of Jason, they sought to bring them forth to the people. And when they found them not, they dragged Jason and certain brethren before the rulers of the city, crying, These that have turned the world upside down are come hither also; whom Jason hath received: and these all act contrary to the decrees of Cæsar, saying that there is another king, one Jesus. And they troubled the multitude and the rulers of the city, when they heard

**these things. And when they had taken security from
Jason and the rest, they let them go.—Acts 17: 1-9.**

"That Christ is our ultimate end, and that only through
Him can we attain salvation"—in these words Savonarola
summed up his own faith. But it was not the saviour-
hood of Christ so much as His kingship that Savonarola
emphasized most deeply in his dealings with the Florentines. However he might have placed Christ in his theology, the more important matter is the part which he
assigned to Christ in the practical affairs and the common
life of Florence. We cannot but be impressed by the
very direct way in which he sought to reestablish Christ
in a definite relation to the city and its people. In a
sermon which he preached in 1494, after the establishment
of the new government, he announced that "it is the
Lord's will to give a new head to the city of Florence";
and after keeping the people in suspense for some time, he
cried, *"The new head is Jesus Christ. He seeks to become
your king."*

The idea caught the imagination of the Florentines
and they went out into the streets shouting, "Long live
Christ our king."

In a poem written by Savonarola, he speaks of "Jesus,
King of Florence," and it was around this point that his
thought at the time chiefly moved. On a certain Palm
Sunday, a service for children was held in the Cathedral
prior to a procession; and after speaking to the children
awhile, Savonarola turned to the men and women present
and cried, "Florence, behold! This is the Lord of the
Universe and would fain be thine. Wilt thou have Him
for thy king?" And the multitude answered, "Long live
Christ our king!"

Ninth Week, Seventh Day

**If there is therefore any comfort in Christ, if any
consolation of love, if any fellowship of the Spirit, if**

any tender mercies and compassions, fulfil ye my joy, that ye be of the same mind, having the same love, being of one accord, of one mind; doing nothing through faction or through vainglory, but in lowliness of mind each counting other better than himself; not looking each of you to his own things, but each of you also to the things of others. Have this mind in you, which was also in Christ Jesus: who, being in the form of God, counted it not a prize to be on an equality with God, but emptied himself, taking the form of a servant, being made in the likeness of men; and being found in fashion as a man, he humbled himself, becoming obedient even unto death, yea, the death of the cross. Wherefore also God highly exalted him, and gave unto him the name which is above every name; that in the name of Jesus every knee should bow, of things in heaven and things on earth and things under the earth, and that every tongue should confess that Jesus Christ is Lord, to the glory of God the Father.—Phil. 2: 1-11.

This, then, is the crowning thought of Savonarola— the absolute and unquestioned sovereignty of Jesus in the heart of the individual and the community. We can afford to pass by our prophet's theology. The intellectual confusion of his time, the conflict of tradition and liberty in his own mind, the tremendous and unbroken whirl into which circumstances forced him in his later years in Florence—these things make it impossible for him to evolve a self-consistent philosophy. But as we follow the man through the fever of those tumultuous years, as we see him essaying statecraft, there emerges a great principle which was never for a moment clouded or obscured—the supreme lordship of Christ over soul and city. Though schooled in an atmosphere of tradition, a child of the middle ages, yet the stirring events of Florentine history call him away from the doctrinal baggage of the schools and the exaggerated ceremonialism of the Church to the central spiritual reality of the Gospel. He was "a reformer before the Reformation." Not yet sufficiently mature to break away formally from the Roman system, nevertheless he heralded not uncertainly that great movement which a generation after his death was to revolutionize western Europe. Martin Luther was fifteen years of age at the time of Savonarola's death; and it was the tattered banner of revolt that the Florentine prophet had laid down too prematurely in 1498 which Luther raised in 1517, when he nailed his "theses" to the door of the Castle Church in Wittenberg, the first act in the drama of the Reformation.

Savonarola has left us for his monument the thought of Jesus as the great overlord of our corporate life. In these democratic days there is a growing sense of the incongruity of conceiving Jesus under terms of secular monarchy. But what was in Savonarola's mind is plain. He meant that our legislation shall be conceived in His spirit, that it shall be enacted and administered along the lines of His will, and that our public bodies, from Parliament and Congress down to the veriest subcommittee of parish councillors or selectmen, shall sit as it were in His presence. Let His will be the touchstone of our enactments, let His principles become the fundamentals of civic and national life, let His character become the citizen's ideal. Thus Savonarola, though he be dead, yet speaketh; and this generation, God knows, needs to listen to him.

SUGGESTIONS FOR THOUGHT AND DISCUSSION

It would be worth while to test the statement that the prophet's first word is *"Repent,"* by reference to Isaiah, Amos, Hosea, and John the Baptist.

Repentance and penitence are often supposed to be the same thing; they are, however, different. How are we to distinguish between them?

Why is the term *King* somewhat unconvincing when we apply it to Jesus? Can you suggest any other term which will retain the spiritual idea implied in kingship, but which is devoid of the notion of authority imposed from without?

CHAPTER X

The Prophet of Humanity— Mazzini

(1805—1872)

The prophet has almost always been a patriot; but his patriotism has been of a distinct order. The blatant assumption of superiority over other peoples, an inflated national pride—these things and such as these which sometimes pass for patriotism bear the name falsely. The true patriotism has other attributes. In its essence it is a passionate love for one's nation, its traditions, and its institutions, joined to a profound faith in its possibilities and in its specific mission in the plan of history. It is not at all akin to that selfish and exclusive temper which regards the securing of certain material goods for a people as a worthy end in itself; on the contrary, it seeks such advantages as will enable the nation to fill its own place in the larger life of the race.

The patriot-prophet always appears at a time when his own country is degenerating and becoming incapable of making its own contribution to the life of the world. He starts by seeing what Jesus once saw and feeling as He then felt—"when he saw the multitudes, he was moved with compassion for them, because they were distressed and scattered, as sheep not having a shepherd." The putrescence of national life, the disintegration of its social bonds—these things weigh heavily on his soul, and he emerges out of the wilderness or the cloister into the highways and the city streets with a great call to repentance. His one passion is to stay the degeneracy, to snatch his people from the perilous incline down which they are sliding to destruction, and to set them again upon the path which they have forsaken and which alone can lead them in safety to their own place in the manifold economy of God.

The Italy of Mazzini's youth was no less broken and distressed than that of Dante or Savonarola. Metternich, the Austrian statesman, had sneered at Italy as merely "a geographical expression," and the description was in fact not untrue. That dream of a united Italy which Dante had dared to dream five hundred years before was still in the clouds. It was to this ideal that Mazzini devoted himself while yet a young man; for it he lived and suffered and wrought. Though the republic in which he had hoped to see Italy united was never established, he nevertheless lived to see Italy a nation, settling down to order its new-found life on lines which would enable it to stand unashamed in the councils of Europe and to make its own contribution to the enrichment of the common life of man. Mazzini, unlike his friend Ruffini, was not permitted to die for Italy; he was compelled to do that more difficult thing—to *live* for his country. In one of his essays he quotes Lamennais, that great French lover of liberty: "Faith demands Action, not tears; it demands of us the power of sacrifice, sole origin of our salvation. It seeks Christians capable of looking down upon the world from on high and facing its fatigues without fear; Christians capable of saying, *'We will die for this';* above all, Christians capable of saying, *'We will live for this.'*" Such an one was Mazzini himself.

[A good collection of Mazzini's essays may be obtained in a volume called by the title of his greatest essay, "The Duties of Man," in Everyman's Library. The volume also contains an excellent biographical introduction.]

DAILY READINGS

Tenth Week, First Day

And what shall I more say? For the time will fail me
if I tell of Gideon, Barak, Samson, Jephthah; of David
and Samuel and the prophets: who through faith subdued
kingdoms, wrought righteousness, obtained promises,
stopped the mouths of lions, quenched the power of fire,
escaped the edge of the sword, from weakness were made
strong, waxed mighty in war, turned to flight armies of
aliens. Women received their dead by a resurrection:
and others were tortured, not accepting their deliverance;
that they might obtain a better resurrection: and others
had trial of mockings and scourgings, yea, moreover of
bonds and imprisonment: they were stoned, they were
sawn asunder, they were tempted, they were slain with
the sword: they went about in sheepskins, in goatskins;
being destitute, afflicted, evil entreated (of whom the
world was not worthy), wandering in deserts and mountains and caves, and the holes of the earth. And these
all, having had witness borne to them through their
faith, received not the promise, God having provided
some better thing concerning us, that apart from us they
should not be made perfect.—Heb. 11: 32-40.

It was no inspiring spectacle that Italy presented to
the eyes of the young Mazzini. There was no national
vitality. The people were plunged into a gross materialism, where they were not wholly buried in a profound indifference. The revolutionary society of the Carbonari,
which Mazzini joined, was zealous enough for Italian
independence; but its spirit was utilitarian and its methods
altogether opportunist. But Mazzini himself was neither
the one nor the other. "I believed," he says of himself,
"that the great problem of the day was a religious problem, to which all other questions were secondary." "The
people," he wrote in his great manifesto, "Faith and the
Future" (1835), "lack faith . . . the faith that arouses
the multitudes, faith in their own destiny, in their own
mission and in the mission of the epoch; the faith that
fights and prays; the faith that enlightens and bids men

advance fearlessly in the ways of God and humanity, with
the sword of the people in their hand, the religion of the
people in their heart, and the future of the people in their
soul."

Faith, in Mazzini's view, was essentially the power of
"seeing the invisible," of deriving inspiration from its
eternal sources in the unseen. He had little patience with
the devious ways and the compromising spirit of the conventional statecraft: the redemption of Italy must be
sought along other lines. Her soul must be raised from
the dead. This was possible only by calling upon her
people as another prophet had done before him, to a nation
equally apathetic, to "lift up their eyes on high." Mazzini
broke away from the revolutionary spirit which cherished
no ideals higher than that of the pocket or the stomach,
and preached to a people held in the deadly grip of an
arid materialism, the old gospel that "man shall not
live by bread alone, but by every word that proceedeth
out of the mouth of God"—by which he proved himself
to belong to "the goodly fellowship of the prophets."

Tenth Week, Second Day

The word that Isaiah the son of Amoz saw concerning
Judah and Jerusalem. And it shall come to pass in the
latter days, that the mountain of the Lord's house shall
be established in the top of the mountains, and shall be
exalted above the hills; and all nations shall flow unto
it. And many peoples shall go and say, Come ye, and
let us go up to the mountain of the Lord, to the house
of the God of Jacob; and he will teach us of his ways,
and we will walk in his paths: for out of Zion shall go
forth the law, and the word of the Lord from Jerusalem.
And he shall judge between the nations, and shall reprove
many peoples: and they shall beat their swords into
plowshares, and their spears into pruninghooks: nation
shall not lift up sword against nation, neither shall they
learn war any more.—Isa. 2: 1-4.

Mazzini's early agitations ended disastrously for him;
he suffered a long exile full of strange vicissitudes.

Nevertheless, he preached his gospel in season and out
of season; and by many devices he secured its propa-
gation in Italy. His exile, however, served him in good
stead. It was not Italy alone that was beginning to be
restless under chains. Europe was seething with the
spirit of revolution; and both England and France became
sanctuaries for many, like Mazzini himself, who were
fugitive from their own countries. In France that brave
priest, Lamennais, was preaching revolutionary doctrine
with the same religious passion as Mazzini, and the
European ferment opened Mazzini's eyes to the true
nature of his problem. It gave him a truer perspective
than he would otherwise have had; so that he became the
prophet not of a nation only but of a whole continent.
He saw on the broad plain of European history what he
saw in little in Italy. This did not in the least weaken
the intensity of his feeling for Italy. On the contrary,
it deepened it, for it was in and through Italy that he
hoped to see accomplished that synthesis of the European
peoples which would be the new birth of man. It is a
commonplace of history and biography that Rome has a
glamor which profoundly affects all minds that are sensitive to its atmosphere and its traditions. Lord Morley
has told us how great a revolution was wrought in
Gladstone's mind and religious outlook by his first visit
to Rome. The same spell was upon Mazzini. "God
chose Rome," he says, "as the interpreter of His design
among the nations. Twice she has given unity to the
world; she will bestow it a third time and forever." The
course of history seems to have drifted away from the
channel of Mazzini's anticipations; but it is none the
less important for our understanding of Mazzini that
we should remember that he looked to Rome for the
enunciation of the new idea, the message of the new
epoch, which was to transform the European jungle into
a vast commonwealth bound together by a common religious ideal.

The Old Testament prophet looked forward to the day when "the mountain of the house of Jehovah" should be exalted above all the mountains and when the nations would pour into it as their common world-metropolis. But upon neither Jerusalem nor Rome has that distinction yet fallen: and it does not appear likely that it ever will. Still, we are plainly drawing nearer the day when the substance if not the form of these prophetic dreams is coming within hail of realization. The League of Nations may be but the framework of that new unity of man for which Mazzini looked.

Tenth Week, Third Day

For as the body is one, and hath many members, and all the members of the body, being many, are one body; so also is Christ. For in one Spirit were we all baptized into one body, whether Jews or Greeks, whether bond or free; and were all made to drink of one Spirit. For the body is not one member, but many. If the foot shall say, Because I am not the hand, I am not of the body; it is not therefore not of the body. And if the ear shall say, Because I am not the eye, I am not of the body; it is not therefore not of the body. If the whole body were an eye, where were the hearing? If the whole were hearing, where were the smelling? But now hath God set the members each one of them in the body, even as it pleased him. And if they were all one member, where were the body?—I Cor. 12: 12-19.

The message of the nineteenth century, according to Mazzini, was to be "synthesis" or "association."

He held that the Protestant Reformation had established finally the principle of individual rights. It was the revolt of the individual mind and conscience against the tyranny of a corrupt and materialistic ecclesiastical system. He further believed that the French Revolution was the "political translation" of the Protestant Reformation; yet he was not inclined to regard the French Revolution with the hot approval that was common among the revolutionary minds of his time. For he said that its exaggerated emphasis upon the principle of individualism had led to its inevitable conclusion in the Empire and the despotism of Napoleon. It is right, he maintained, that all persons should be free; but if you have only freedom, then you have competition and strife. The principle of individual liberty must be balanced by another; and to this other, Mazzini gave the name of "association" or "synthesis," which, of course, means just "getting together." This is the reason why Mazzini emphasized not personal rights but personal duties; and it were always well for us to hear more of duties than of rights. Emphasis on our rights tends to separate us, to set us against one another; but emphasis on duties will help to unite us, to bind us together.

It was Mazzini's belief and hope that the mission of the nineteenth century was to establish this principle of association in national and international life. The previous epoch had shown what society owed to the individual; the nineteenth century would show what the individual owed to society. Up to a certain point, Mazzini's foresight was justified. While, in England at least, the trend of legislation in the first half of the nineteenth century had been individualistic, a process of securing individual rights, in the latter half the tendency was collectivistic, that is to say, it expressed the collective action of the community in defense of its members against exploitation, by means of Factory Acts, Truck Acts, and the like. Still better evidence of the truth of Mazzini's prediction is to be found in the appearance and growth of what we call "the social consciousness" and the sense of corporate duty and service. Says Lowell,

"Slowly the Bible of the race is writ,"

and every age adds its own chapter. The nineteenth century did not write out this chapter as fully as Mazzini had anticipated; but it at least began it. And the social movement is today the most significant fact of our common life.

In preaching this doctrine of association, Mazzini was, of course, only amplifying that old word, "Ye are members one of another."

Tenth Week, Fourth Day

Behold, a king shall reign in righteousness, and princes shall rule in judgement. And a man shall be as an hiding place from the wind, and a covert from the tempest; as rivers of water in a dry place, as the shadow of a great rock in a weary land. And the eyes of them that see shall not be dim, and the ears of them that hear shall hearken. The heart also of the rash shall understand knowledge, and the tongue of the stammerers shall be ready to speak plainly. The vile person shall be no more called liberal, nor the churl said to be bountiful. For the vile person will speak villany, and his heart will work iniquity, to practise profaneness, and to utter error against the Lord, to make empty the soul of the hungry, and to cause the drink of the thirsty to fail. The instruments also of the churl are evil: he deviseth wicked devices to destroy the meek with lying words, even when the needy speaketh right. But the liberal deviseth liberal things; and in liberal things shall he continue. . . . Then judgement shall dwell in the wilderness, and righteousness shall abide in the fruitful field. And the work of righteousness shall be peace; and the effect of righteousness quietness and confidence for ever.—Isa. 32: 1-8, 16, 17.

"For God and Humanity"—these were the words which Mazzini inscribed on the banner which he carried so long and so bravely. He believed, in spite of all appearance to the contrary, that the passing of time meant surely and certainly the unfolding of the divine purpose in man. The cause of God and man are one. "Man," says Dr. Garvie, "must be conceived as a means towards God's

ends, but not as merely a means, but a means in such
sense that he fulfils his own ends in realizing God's."
To this statement Mazzini would have subscribed. Starting from a belief in the inviolability of human personality,
Mazzini asserts that the individual has "his own mission
of citizenship within the sphere of the Fatherland."
But the Fatherland, while itself the home of an association of individuals, is in its turn a unit in the larger
association of the peoples, and Mazzini asserts that all
progress depends upon a frank and practical acceptance
of this principle. Humanity must henceforward move
in the mass. It is through the mass movement of the
race that the individual is to come into his own; and this
mass movement was to be the next stage in the unfolding
of the divine purpose. That human history, as Carlyle
said, is at bottom the history of certain great men may
be true; it has been the case that God has elevated the
race by means of the giants He has made—and Mazzini
was assuredly among the giants. But it was to be less
so in the future. Mankind would move onward as a
whole. Not indeed that any past achievement is rejected.
"Before us is the evolution of a future in which the two
eternal elements of every organization, the individual
and humanity, liberty and association, will be harmonized;
in which one whole synthesis, a veritable religious
formula, will without suppressing any in favor of the
rest, embrace all the revelations of progress, all the holy
ideas that have been successively transmitted to us by
providential design."

Because God was "in the beginning," Mazzini believed that, in spite of all the reactions and setbacks
which history records, the principle of progress had been
permanently active in the world. He condemns what he
calls the "circular movement" school of history, which
holds that because human nature is always and everywhere the same, history must of necessity go on for ever
repeating itself. Newman has expressed the idea:

"The world has cycles in its course
  That once has been is acted o'er again,
Not by some fated law that need appal
  Our faith or binds our deed as with a chain,
But by men's separate sins which blended still
  The same bad round fulfil."

That history does, though it need not, repeat itself is Newman's thought; but Mazzini denied that history ever repeated itself at all. Parallels there may be, but never the *same* bad round. The increasing purpose may be retarded, but is never altogether stayed; and, notwithstanding his own reverses and disillusionments, Mazzini believed that nothing could prevent the ultimate triumph of the cause of God and man. In one place Mazzini tells the story of Galileo before the Inquisition. The astronomer had recanted, had withdrawn his detestable heresy that the sun was stationary and that the earth moved around it. But as he was leaving the court, he turned and cried, "And yet it moves!" "Child of humanity!" cries Mazzini, "raise thy brow to the sun of God and read upon its heavens, *it moves!* Faith and Action! The future is ours!"

Tenth Week, Fifth Day

This is my commandment, that ye love one another, even as I have loved you. Greater love hath no man than this, that a man lay down his life for his friends. Ye are my friends, if ye do the things which I command you. No longer do I call you servants; for the servant knoweth not what his lord doeth: but I have called you friends; for all things that I heard from my Father I have made known unto you. Ye did not choose me, but I chose you, and appointed you, that ye should go and bear fruit, and that your fruit should abide: that whatsoever ye shall ask of the Father in my name, he may give it you. These things I command you, that ye may love one another.—John 15: 12-17.

It has been necessary in order to understand the place

that Jesus occupied in Mazzini's mind to sketch in some detail the vast sweep of Mazzini's own faith and hope for the world. His vision includes the whole race; and his mission was to preach its unity. Despite all manner of discouragement, he went on preaching, and that in no uncertain voice. And if we would find the secret of this conquering optimism, we must turn to a great passage in "Faith and the Future" which is the most elaborate statement which Mazzini gives of his religious faith. After describing the state of utter hopelessness and darkness into which the world had fallen under the Roman Empire, when "philosophy had sunk first into skepticism, then into epicureanism, then into subtlety and words, when poetry had been transformed into satire," he goes on:

"Yet there were moments when men were terror-stricken by the solitude around them, and trembled at their isolation. They ran to embrace the cold and naked statues of their once venerated gods, to implore of them a spark of moral life, a ray of faith, even an illusion. They departed, their prayers unheard, with despair in their hearts and blasphemy on their lips. . . . Yet this was not the death agony of the world. It was the conclusion of one evolution of the world which had reached its ultimate expression. A great epoch was exhausted, and passing away to give place to another, the first utterances of which had already been heard in the north and which wanted but the *Initiator* to be revealed.

He came—the soul the most full of love, the most sacredly virtuous, the most deeply inspired by God and by the future, that men have yet seen on earth—Jesus. He bent over the corpse of the dead world and whispered a word of faith. Over the clay that had lost all of man but the movement and the form, He uttered words until then unknown, *love, sacrifice, a heavenly origin*. And the dead arose. A new life circulated through the clay which philosophy had in vain tried to reanimate. From that corpse arose the Christian world, the world of liberty and equality. From that clay arose the true Man, the image of God, the precursor of humanity.

Christ expired. All He had asked of mankind wherewith to save them, says Lamennais, was a Cross whereon to die. But ere He died, He had announced the glad tidings to the people; to those who asked of Him whence He had received it, He answered, 'From God the Father.' From the height of His Cross, he had invoked Him twice. Therefore upon the Cross did His victory begin and still does it endure."

Tenth Week, Sixth Day

I am the true vine, and my Father is the husbandman. Every branch in me that beareth not fruit, he taketh it away: and every branch that beareth fruit, he cleanseth it, that it may bear more fruit. Already ye are clean because of the word which I have spoken unto you. Abide in me, and I in you. As the branch cannot bear fruit of itself, except it abide in the vine; so neither can ye, except ye abide in me. I am the vine, ye are the branches: He that abideth in me, and I in him, the same beareth much fruit: for apart from me ye can do nothing. If a man abide not in me, he is cast forth as a branch, and is withered; and they gather them, and cast them into the fire, and they are burned. If ye abide in me, and my words abide in you, ask whatsoever ye will, and it shall be done unto you. Herein is my Father glorified, that ye bear much fruit; and so shall ye be my disciples. —John 15: 1-8.

It would be idle to pretend that Mazzini's view of Jesus and the Cross can be squared with the traditional doctrines of the Church; but here is a frank recognition of the unique place which Jesus fills in human history. There is, however, something more. Properly understood, the passage quoted in yesterday's reading suggests the conception of Jesus as "the representative man." It is not very important that Mazzini does not speak theologically; but it is plain that to him Jesus is the epitome of humanity, and Calvary a summary of history.

That linking of God and man which Jesus in life,
supremely in death, accomplished, was not alone the
promise but the sure guarantee of human fulfilment—
for man's end is in God. In what Jesus has done we
see the pledge of what man will be, and by that same
path of love and sacrifice which led Christ to Calvary
shall humanity at least reach God. Christ is the captain
of the salvation not alone of men but of Man. The path
He trod is the highway of the eternal purpose. "We
advance," says Mazzini, "encouraged by the sacred promise of Jesus"—the promise not only spoken in words but
explicit in His life and work; and this promise was the
sure destiny of man in God. He "bestowed upon the
human race that sublime formula of *brotherhood*," but, in
Mazzini's view, brotherhood was not an end but a means
to an end. He believed that men cannot relate themselves rightly to God save through "collective humanity."
We shall see the glory of God when we see it together.
This is the truth that Christianity recognizes in its
emphasis upon "the communion of saints"; man realizes
himself only in fellowship, and it is therefore only so
far as he consciously participates in the forward movement of the race towards the widest possible fellowship,
that he can bring himself fully into union with God.
Mazzini did not at any time deny the possibility of
personal communion with God; indeed, more than once,
he bade men pray; but personal religion was not his
peculiar message. He was charged to declare to men
that it is only through conscious and deliberate identification of oneself with the body of mankind that the union
of God and man—man's chief end and God's chief aim
—can in the end be secured.

Tenth Week, Seventh Day

But now put ye also away all these; anger, wrath,
malice, railing, shameful speaking out of your mouth:
lie not one to another; seeing that ye have put off the

old man with his doings, and have put on the new man, which is being renewed unto knowledge after the image of him that created him: where there cannot be Greek and Jew, circumcision and uncircumcision, barbarian, Scythian, bondman, freeman: but Christ is all, and in all.

Put on therefore, as God's elect, holy and beloved, a heart of compassion, kindness, humility, meekness, long-suffering; forbearing one another, and forgiving each other, if any man have a complaint against any; even as the Lord forgave you, so also do ye: and above all these things put on love, which is the bond of perfectness. And let the peace of Christ rule in your hearts, to the which also ye were called in one body; and be ye thankful.—Col. 3: 8-15.

Christ in his relation to collective man—that is the contribution that Mazzini makes to our thought of Jesus. The Italian prophet had an eye and a heart for the multitude; and the sins and imperfections of the individual were for him merged in the need of the whole. "In contemplating men, say, soldiers, weavers, colliers in a collective body," says Dora Greenwell in her beautiful book "Two Friends," "we feel the heart drawn out in a deepened sympathy which none among them as individuals would command. . . . Does it not arise from being brought within the influences of the broad tendencies of humanity where individual limitations disappear, swept away by the force of the current? Such moments seem to say to us, 'Behold the Man'; they are baptismal and endue the soul with much strength. . . . Passion, interest, caprice, belong to the individual; and in this surely lies the strength of the saying *Vox Populi, Vox Dei,* that a number of persons acting together are naturally less under the control of circumstance, 'this world's unspiritual God,' and less fettered by prejudice than the few. Also we know that in every lump there is a leaven of nobleness—some, perhaps many, tender and truthful souls. The heart of a people, if it could but speak, is *always in its right place.* . . . And it is this, too, which gives such a double dye to all sins

against national freedom, which is but the expression
of a people's life. If it is a crime to slay a man, what
must it be to strike against a nation, to kill a man in
his organic life? . . . To break faith with a nation is
to break a deeper trust, to blight a fuller hope than
can be involved in any treachery towards the individual.
Who is this, the true Antichrist, he that denieth the
Father and the Son, but the absolutist and the tyrant?
We are surely not sufficiently sensible of the atheism
involved in the deep iniquity of oppression. *It is the
denial of God through the denial of Man."*

This is Mazzini's own religion and philosophy; only
he goes still farther. For he goes beyond national
frontiers and believes that the time will come when
"the lips of patriots will cease to utter the word *foreigner*
as a term of reproach, which, in men calling themselves
brothers, is a blasphemy against the Cross of Christ."
On Calvary Mazzini saw the pledge and promise of
human solidarity, because there he saw the representative man in perfect union with God. The Cross of
Christ is the seal of human brotherhood, the triumph
of the Cross the earnest of that coming synthesis, that
"perfect man," in whom "there cannot be Greek and
Jew, circumcision and uncircumcision, barbarian,
Scythian, bondman, freeman: but Christ is all, and in all."

SUGGESTIONS FOR THOUGHT AND DISCUSSION

Is patriotism consistent with Christianity? Can you
find any evidence to justify us in saying that Jesus was
a patriot?

Do you think Jesus would have believed in a "league
of nations"? If so, what are the grounds on which you
think so?

Mazzini's great idea was that *liberty* and *association*
must always go together. Can you recall any sayings of
Jesus which suggest that He also believed this?

CHAPTER XI

The Prophet of Service—John Ruskin

(1819—1900)

Ruskin, like Browning and Tennyson, is one of the peaks of nineteenth century Britain. But the intellectual storms which fell upon the poets seem on the whole to have passed the prophet by. This is, no doubt, due to the circumstance that Ruskin's chief interest lay in the province of Art; and though this province was visited by tempest, it was from another source and of another kind. It was in a sense a domestic controversy concerning principles and methods in Art. Roughly it may be said that, apart from questions of technique, Ruskin's great mission was to proclaim the sovereignty of truth and righteousness in Art as it had been Savonarola's mission in the State. It must, however, be remembered in this connection—so fundamentally one is life—that Ruskin's interest in Art led him to become a preacher of economic change. Like his great contemporary, William Morris, he saw that the banishment of beauty from life was the result of the prevailing commercial and industrial order; and he came to believe in the need of drastic economic reformation as a condition of restoring beauty to life. His economic philosophy he stated in a little volume, "Unto This Last," which was much derided by the orthodox economists when it appeared, but which has since exercised a profound influence upon economic thought. It is no exaggeration to say that the humanizing of economic science in our time owes its chief impetus to Ruskin's work.

Ruskin's most important works are treatises on the fine arts, the chief being "Modern Painters," "The Seven Lamps of Architecture," "The Stones of Venice," and they owe their power not less to the beauty of their literary composition than to their subject-matter and the treatment of it. It is worth noticing that Ruskin attributed the acknowledged beauty of his English to his familiarity with the Authorized Version of the Bible.

"When people read," wrote Ruskin in "Modern Painters," " 'the law came by Moses but grace and truth through Jesus Christ,' do they suppose it means that the law was ungracious or untrue? The law was given for a foundation, the grace (or mercy) and truth for fulfilment; the whole forming one glorious trinity of judgment, mercy, and truth." Years later Ruskin reproduced this passage in "Frondes Agrestes," and added a footnote: "A great deal of the presumption and narrowness caused by my having been bred in the evangelical schools, and which now fill me with shame and distress in re-reading 'Modern Painters,' is, to my present mind, atoned for by the accurate thinking by which I broke my way through to the great truth expressed in this passage, which all my later works, without exception, have been directed to maintain and illustrate." We may question even now whether Ruskin correctly expounds the Scripture passage which he quotes; but there can be no question that we have here the real clue to Ruskin's philosophy of life.

To think justly, to love mercy, to speak and act truth —without these there can be neither goodness nor greatness, in Art or in Literature, in the State or in individual life. Neglect these things, and degeneracy sets in. In "The Stones of Venice" Ruskin has shown how the period of Venetian prosperity and the golden age of its

art was also the time of its devotion to high moral
ideals; but when the moral standards became obscure,
and "in the ingenuity of indulgence, in the varieties of
vanity, Venice surpassed the cities of Christendom as of
old she had surpassed them in fortitude and devotion,"
her art declined, and "by the inner burning of her own
passions, as fatal as the fiery rain of Gomorrah, she
was consumed from her place among the nations; and
her ashes are choking the channels of the dead salt sea."
This is a true philosophy of life and history.

[Most of Ruskin's works are now available in a cheap
   form in Everyman's Library.]

DAILY READINGS

Eleventh Week, First Day

Lord, who shall sojourn in thy tabernacle?
Who shall dwell in thy holy hill?
He that walketh uprightly, and worketh righteousness,
And speaketh truth in his heart.
He that slandereth not with his tongue,
Nor doeth evil to his friend,
Nor taketh up a reproach against his neighbour.
In whose eyes a reprobate is despised;
But he honoureth them that fear the Lord.
He that sweareth to his own hurt, and changeth not.
He that putteth not out his money to usury,
Nor taketh reward against the innocent.
He that doeth these things shall never be moved.
                                        —Psalm 15.

John Ruskin was essentially a religious soul, and to
him the essence of religion was communion with God.
But communion with God requires two conditions.
The first is that man shall possess moral qualities cor-
responding to those of the divine nature. "It is only,"
says Ruskin, "to a nature capable of truth, desirous of
it, distinguishing it, feeding upon it, that revelation is

possible. There can be none to a brute or to a fiend.
In so far, therefore, as you love truth and live therein,
in so far revelation can exist for you; and in so far,
your mind is the image of God." This is simply an
expansion of an older word—"Blessed are the pure in
heart, for they shall see God." It is in the measure that
truth and justice and love are our own personal qualities that we shall be able to receive and apprehend the
word in which God reveals Himself. The image of God
within is "defiled, if you will; broken, if you will; all
but effaced, if you will, by death and the shadow of it."
For all that it is "a mirror wherein may be seen darkly
the image of the mind of God."

The second condition of communion with God is that
God's mind should be expressed in terms that our finite
minds càn grasp. "In order to make this communion
possible, the Deity has stooped from His throne and has
not only in the person of the Son taken upon Him the
veil of our human flesh, but in the person of the Father
taken upon Him the veil of our human thoughts and
permitted us to conceive Him simply and clearly as a
loving Father and Friend, a Being to be walked with
and reasoned with, to be moved by our entreaties, to be
angered by our rebellion, alienated by our coldness,
pleased by our love, and glorified by our labour, and
finally to be beheld in immediate and active presence in
all the powers and changes of creation. This conception
of God, which is the child's, is evidently the only one
which can be universal, and therefore the only one
which *for us* can be true."

It is clear that Ruskin accepted the truth of the Incarnation fully; and again and again he insists upon it
as the central fact of the Gospel. Sometimes he discovers a meaning in it which may not commend itself to
us; but, taking it altogether, there is a wealth and variety
in Ruskin's interpretation of Jesus which may not easily
be fully expressed in a small compass.

Eleventh Week, Second Day

If then ye were raised together with Christ, seek the things that are above, where Christ is, seated on the right hand of God. Set your mind on the things that are above, not on the things that are upon the earth. For ye died, and your life is hid with Christ in God. When Christ, who is our life, shall be manifested, then shall ye also with him be manifested in glory.—Col. 3: 1-4.

Ruskin had been brought up in the straitest evangelicalism—a phase of Christian thought which, because it was a protest against both the dry liberalism and the formal High-Churchmanship of the late eighteenth and early nineteenth centuries, cast itself into forms more rigid than a larger outlook could possibly consent to. While Ruskin deplored the narrowness which this type of Christianity had induced in him, and he had in many respects departed from it, yet he remained true to its essential features to the end. We have seen his confession that while he was writing "Modern Painters," he was still under the influence of the older ideas; but he shows in "Praeterita" that even at the end of his life what was fundamental in his early inheritance was still with him. "What a child," he says, "cannot understand of Christianity no man need try to. . . . The total meaning was and is that God who made earth and its creatures took at a certain time on the earth the flesh and the form of man; in that flesh sustained the pain and died the death of the creature He had made; rose after death into glorious human life; and when the date of the human race is ended, will return in visible human form and render to every man according to his work. Christianity is the belief in and love of God thus manifested."

There is no great disparity between this and his earlier view. Yet in one important respect Ruskin departed materially from his first faith. The evangelicalism in which he had been bred had chiefly emphasized the *death*

of Jesus. Ruskin shifts the larger emphasis to the *risen*
Christ. This does not mean that he did not attach
great significance to the death of Jesus, but he felt
rather the immense and wonderful significance of the
thought that Jesus lives today, and that the chief business of His disciples is to be in a living and immediate
obedience to Him. In the "Lectures on Art," he deplores
the wasted time and the wasted emotion of the tender
and delicate women of Christendom, when they have
been called "through the four arts of eloquence, music,
painting, and sculpture," to contemplate "the bodily pain,
long passed" of "the Master who is not dead and who is
not now fainting under His Cross, but requiring us to
take up ours." Speaking of the sculpture on the great
central porch of Amiens Cathedral, he says, "Christ
never appears, or is for a moment thought of, as the
crucified or the dead; but as the Incarnate Word, as the
present Friend, as the Prince of Peace on earth, and
as the Everlasting King in heaven. What His life *is,*
what His commands *are,* and what His judgment *will be,*
are the things taught here; not what He once did, or
what He once suffered, but what He is now doing and
what He requires us to do. That is the pure joyful les-
son of Christianity, and the fall from that faith and
the corruption of its abortive practice may be summed
up briefly as the habitual contemplation of Christ's death
instead of His life: the substitution of His past suffering
for our present duty."

But is this, after all, anything different from St. Paul's
thought: "For if . . . we were reconciled to God through
the death of his Son, much more, being reconciled, shall
we be saved by his life"?

Eleventh Week, Third Day

Wherefore if any man is in Christ, he is a new creature: the old things are passed away; behold, they are
become new. But all things are of God, who reconciled

us to himself through Christ, and gave unto us the
ministry of reconciliation; to wit, that God was in
Christ reconciling the world unto himself, not reckon-
ing unto them their trespasses, and having committed
unto us the word of reconciliation.

We are ambassadors therefore on behalf of Christ,
as though God were intreating by us: we beseech you on
behalf of Christ, be ye reconciled to God. Him who
knew no sin he made to be sin on our behalf; that we
might become the righteousness of God in him.—II
Cor. 5: 17-21.

Ruskin's emphasis on the living Christ does not lead
him to undervalue the gospel history. He speaks of
"three facts, without assurance of which all faith is
vain—namely, that Christ died, that He rose again, and
that He ascended into heaven, there to prepare a place
for His elect." Indeed, it is only from what we know
of the historical Jesus that we can gain any confident
knowledge of the living Christ; and in this connection
Ruskin insists strongly upon the real and eternal manhood
of Christ. The glorified Christ is no other than the
man Jesus—the same yesterday, today, and forever. "Our
preachers," he complains, "are continually trying in all
manner of subtle ways to explain the union of the
Divinity with the Manhood, an explanation which certainly involves first their being able to describe the
nature of the Deity itself or, in plain words, to apprehend God. They never can explain, in any one particular,
the union of the natures; they only succeed in weaken-
ing the faith of their hearers as to the entireness of
either. The thing they have to do is precisely the contrary to this—to insist upon the entireness of both. We
never think of Christ enough as God, never enough
as Man: the instinctive habit of our minds being always
to miss of the divinity, and the reasoning and enforced
habit to miss of the humanity. We are afraid to har-
bour in our own hearts, or to utter in the hearing of
others, any thought of our Lord as hungering, tired,

sorrowful, having a human soul, a human will, and
affected by events of human life, as a finite creature is;
and yet one half of the efficiency of His atonement and
the whole of the efficiency of His example depend upon
His having been this to the full"—which is, of course,
uncommonly good sense.

Eleventh Week, Fourth Day

And they constrained him, saying, Abide with us:
for it is toward evening, and the day is now far spent.
And he went in to abide with them. And it came to
pass, when he had sat down with them to meat, he took
the bread, and blessed it, and brake, and gave to them.
And their eyes were opened, and they knew him; and
he vanished out of their sight. And they said one to
another, Was not our heart burning within us, while
he spake to us in the way, while he opened to us the
scriptures? And they rose up that very hour, and
returned to Jerusalem, and found the eleven gathered
together, and them that were with them, saying, The
Lord is risen indeed, and hath appeared to Simon. And
they rehearsed the things that happened in the way,
and how he was known of them in the breaking of the
bread.—Luke 24: 29-35.

The example of the Jesus of history is for His disciples
the law of the Christ of glory. And the commandments
of this law are not merely the words of an ancient
record, but words which come to us straight from the
high throne on which the Living Lord is set. In His
Law is our life. Jesus revealed not only God but man,
and by His life He has shown wherein our life consists.
And just as the Son of Man came to minister, and as
He ministered above all, to the poor, the outcast, and
the broken, so also is our life to consist in such lowliness of service. "Could we," asks our author, "possibly
have had more distinct indication of the purpose of the
Master, first borne by the witness of the shepherds in
a cattle-shed, then by the witness of the person for whom
He had done most and who loved Him best, in the

garden and in gardener's guise, and not known by His
familiar friends till He gave them bread—could it be
told us, I repeat, more definitely by any sign or indication whatsoever that the noblest human life was appointed
to be by the cattle-fold and in the garden, and to be
known as noble in the breaking of bread?" This expression "the breaking of bread" is symbolical throughout Ruskin's works of lowly deeds of mercy, of loving
care for the poor and the spent; and the reward of
those who break bread is that it brings them the vision
of Christ.

This conception of life and discipleship as service is
Ruskin's real gospel and he expands it in various forms.
In "Unto This Last" he says that in every community
there are four great intellectual professions—the soldier's, to defend it; the lawyer's, to secure justice in it;
the pastor's, to teach it; and the merchant's, to provide
for it. And it is the duty of each of these, he says,
"on due occasion to die for it." This requirement of an
absolute devotion of service, stated so uncompromisingly,
is the logic of Ruskin's own view of Christianity and
of Jesus. He who was obedient unto death requires the
same quality of obedience in His followers.

Eleventh Week, Fifth Day

But Mary was standing without at the tomb weeping:
so, as she wept, she stooped and looked into the tomb;
and she beholdeth two angels in white sitting, one at
the head, and one at the feet, where the body of Jesus
had lain. And they say unto her, Woman, why weepest
thou? She saith unto them, Because they have taken
away my Lord, and I know not where they have laid
him. When she had thus said, she turned herself back,
and beholdeth Jesus standing, and knew not that it was
Jesus. Jesus saith unto her, Woman, why weepest thou?
whom seekest thou? She, supposing him to be the
gardener, saith unto him, Sir, if thou hast borne him
hence, tell me where thou hast laid him, and I will take
him away. Jesus saith unto her, Mary. She turneth

herself, and saith unto him in Hebrew, Rabboni; which
is to say, Master. Jesus saith to her, Touch me not;
for I am not yet ascended unto the Father: but go
unto my brethren, and say to them, I ascend unto my
Father and your Father, and my God and your God.—
John 20: 11-17.

This life of service has its own peculiar rewards; re-
fusal of it, its peculiar penalties. "Take Christ at His
literal word, and so sure as His word is true, He will
be known of you in the breaking of bread. Refuse that
servant's duty because it is plain, seek either to serve
God or know Him in any other way, your service will
become mockery of Him and your knowledge darkness."
Ruskin is here simply enforcing the principle which we
have already found in a previous passage: the measure
of our likeness to God is the measure of our apprehension
of Him. It is the same with the understanding of Christ.
"There is only one light by which you can read the life
of Christ—the light of the life which you now lead in
the flesh; and that not the natural life, but the *won* life.
'Nevertheless I live, yet not I, but Christ liveth in me.'"
But the indwelling Christ will through us do the works
of Christ; and in that service is vision. In a passage
in "Sesame and Lilies," where he speaks of the poor
and helpless children of England, "the feeble florets,
with all their fresh leaves torn and their stems broken,"
he asks, "will you not go down among them nor set them
in order in their little fragrant beds, nor fence them,
in their trembling, from the fierce wind?" And after
quoting Tennyson's lines,

> "Come into the garden, Maud,
> I am here at the gate alone,"

he goes on: "who is it, think you, who stands at the
gate of the sweeter garden, alone, waiting for you?
Did you ever hear not of a Maude but a Madeleine, who
went down to her garden in the dawn and found One

waiting at the gate whom she supposed to be the gardener? Have you not sought Him often; sought Him in vain, all through the night; sought Him in vain at the gate of that old garden where the fiery sword is set? He is never there, but at the gate of *this* garden He is waiting always—waiting to take your hand—ready to see the fruits of the valley, to see whether the vine has flourished and the pomegranate budded."

Eleventh Week, Sixth Day

But when the Son of man shall come in his glory, and all the angels with him, then shall he sit on the throne of his glory: and before him shall be gathered all the nations: and he shall separate them one from another, as the shepherd separateth the sheep from the goats: and he shall set the sheep on his right hand, but the goats on the left. Then shall the King say unto them on his right hand, Come, ye blessed of my Father, inherit the kingdom prepared for you from the foundation of the world: for I was an hungred, and ye gave me meat: I was thirsty, and ye gave me drink: I was a stranger, and ye took me in; naked, and ye clothed me: I was sick, and ye visited me: I was in prison, and ye came unto me. Then shall the righteous answer him, saying, Lord, when saw we thee an hungred, and fed thee? or athirst, and gave thee drink? And when saw we thee a stranger, and took thee in? or naked, and clothed thee? And when saw we thee sick, or in prison, and came unto thee? And the King shall answer and say unto them, Verily I say unto you, Inasmuch as ye did it unto one of these my brethren, even these least, ye did it unto me. Then shall he say also unto them on the left hand, Depart from me, ye cursed, into the eternal fire which is prepared for the devil and his angels: for I was an hungred, and ye gave me no meat: I was thirsty, and ye gave me no drink: I was a stranger, and ye took me not in; naked, and ye clothed me not; sick, and in prison, and ye visited me not. Then shall they also answer, saying, Lord, when saw we thee an hungred, or athirst, or a stranger, or naked, or sick, or in prison, and did not minister unto thee? Then shall he answer them, saying, Verily I say unto you, Inasmuch as ye did it not unto one of these least, ye did it

not unto me. And these shall go away into eternal punishment: but the righteous into eternal life.—Matt. 25: 31-46.

This thought of meeting Jesus in the service of the broken is, of course, common enough in literature. It is the subject of two of James Russell Lowell's poems, "The Vision of Sir Launfal" and "The Search." In the latter, the poet tells us how he had sought Christ in nature, in the halls of the rich, and in the houses of worship, and, turning from his vain quest into the streets of the city, he saw the prints of bleeding feet:

> "I followed where they led,
>   And in a hovel rude,
> With naught to fence the weather from his head,
>   The King I sought for meekly stood;
>   A naked hungry child
>   Clung round his gracious knee,
> And a poor hunted slave looked up and smiled
>   To bless the smile that set him free;
> New miracles I saw his presence do,
>   No more I knew the hovel bare and poor,
> The gathered chips into a woodpile grew,
>   The broken morsel swelled to goodly store.
> I knelt and wept: my Christ no more I seek.
> His throne is with the outcast and the weak."

"Inasmuch as ye have done it unto the least of these ye have done it unto me." The service of Jesus is the service of the broken and the spent; and for no service is there ampler recompense. "Obey the word (of Christ) in its simplicity, in wholeness of purpose, and serenity of sacrifice . . . and truly you shall receive sevenfold into your bosom in this present life and in the world to come life everlasting. All your knowledge will become to you clear and sure, all your footsteps safe; in the present brightness of domestic life you will foretaste the joy of Paradise, and to your children's children bequeath not only noble fame but endless virtue."

Eleventh Week, Seventh Day

For behold your calling, brethren, how that not many wise after the flesh, not many mighty, not many noble, are called: but God chose the foolish things of the world, that he might put to shame them that are wise; and God chose the weak things of the world, that he might put to shame the things that are strong; and the base things of the world, and the things that are despised, did God choose, yea and the things that are not, that he might bring to nought the things that are: that no flesh should glory before God. But of him are ye in Christ Jesus, who was made unto us wisdom from God, and righteousness and sanctification, and redemption: that, according as it is written, He that glorieth, let him glory in the Lord.—I Cor. 1: 26-31.

Upon this loyal obedience all the good of life hangs. "The strength and joy and height of achievement of any group or race of mankind has, from the day of Christ's nativity to this hour, been in exact proportion to their power of apprehending and honesty in obeying the truth of His Gospel." And the moral obviously is: "Be sure that you are serving Christ, till you are tired and can do no more for that time; and then, even if you have not breath enough left to say 'Master, Master,' with, He will not mind. Begin therefore 'today' . . . to do good for Him—whether you live or die." And to those who thus obey Him, he becomes "all in all." "The early believers knew that the believer who had Christ had all. Did he need fortitude? Christ was his rock. Equity? Christ was his righteousness. Holiness? Christ was his sanctification. Liberty? Christ was his redemption. Temperance? Christ was his ruler. Wisdom? Christ was his light. Truthfulness? Christ was the truth. Charity? Christ was love." Throughout his life he is sustained by Christ, and in that sustenance is perfect satisfaction. "It is enough for Christ's sheep that they find themselves on Christ's shoulders."

Ruskin's Christ is the living and ever sufficient Master, who in grace governs and sustains His servants, whose life is their pattern, whose indwelling is their strength. It is the Christ of whom St. Paul, in Frederic Myers's poem, says:

"Yea, through life, death, through sorrow and through
  sinning,
  Christ shall suffice me, for he hath sufficed;
Christ is the end, for Christ is the beginning,
  Christ the beginning, for the end is Christ."

SUGGESTIONS FOR THOUGHT AND DISCUSSION

Is Ruskin right in saying that the sufferings and death of Jesus have been over-emphasized in the past?

"What a child cannot understand of Christianity no man need try to." Discuss this statement.

What are the "due occasions" on which the lawyer and the merchant should die for their country?

CHAPTER XII

The Universal Jesus

The inquiry upon which we have been engaged could, of course, be continued indefinitely; and some of those who have gone thus far may desire to go yet farther. There is much territory still to be explored in this matter of the personal witness of great souls—more detailed inquiry, for instance, into the witness of the mystics, John Tauler, Brother Lawrence, Thomas à Kempis, Henry Suso, Miguel de Molinos, Richard Rolle of Hampole, and others of this gentle company. We might also examine more closely the place of Jesus in philosophy; and there is a rich vein to be worked out in the region of the social and political consequences of His appearance. Still another approach might be made from the side of "specialist" interpretations of Jesus—for example, the mystical interpretation of the life of Jesus by Miss Evelyn Underhill, the economic interpretation by Dr. Bernard Shaw, the psychological interpretation by Dr. Stanley Hall, and the like. Even the bare mention of these possibilities goes to show the singular distinction of Jesus.

In our present inquiry we have seen from how many different angles men have looked upon Jesus, and under how many aspects men have seen Him. To Dante, He was the glorified Redeemer; to Shelley, the supreme poet and reformer; to William Blake, the incarnation of that divine energy which is for ever creating life and beauty and fellowship; to Browning, the clue to the mystery of the universe; to Tennyson, the divine revealer and interpreter of God and man; to Francis Thompson, the ever-present Lover who will not let us go. To Savonarola, He was the overlord of cities; to Mazzini, the symbol and promise of universal human unity; to John Ruskin, the living Master who puts us all to work and sustains us while we are at it.

And so comes this tremendous question—How does it happen that all these different characters should be ascribed to one person? How could one man fill so many rôles? Of course, it may be answered that each of these people of whom we have inquired may have simply identified his own personal *ideal* with Jesus and found in Jesus what it suited him to find. That may be true, of course, and yet the remarkable fact remains that all these various ideals seemed to sit easily and without strain upon Jesus. We know that other persons have been idealized and deified in history; but none have been treated in this way so consistently and so continuously as Jesus. He seems to stand alone.

Yet there are those who say that Jesus never existed, that He is a fictitious, mythical figure. There may have been once an uncommonly good man in Palestine called Jesus, but he is a very shadowy form. The person we find in the gospels is a composite picture, built up around this obscure individual of whom we can know next to nothing for certain—in which case you have to explain the extraordinary art which clothed this diaphanous figure with so much life that he has imposed himself in this royal and various way upon the generations of men. You are confronted with a choice of two miracles, the miracle of Jesus or the miracle of art. In either case, you have a miracle.

Criticism has its place and office in religion; and it is stupid ignorance that cries out against it. But the danger of criticism is to suppose that its own method covers the whole field. Now the fact is that, because criticism is so preoccupied with the examination of texts

and the scrutiny of details, it is sometimes unable to see
the wood for the trees. Of course, we must avoid the
other danger of not seeing the trees for the wood and
missing the real significance of the exact and scientific
study of the gospels. What we have to remember is that,
when criticism and exegesis have done their work, they
have yet to be submitted to the test of the whole human
impression of Jesus. The study of the total impact of
the person of Jesus upon the whole man is as necessary
for the purpose of securing a just proportion in our
thought of Jesus, as is the minute and microscopic examination of records. It is this study upon which we
have been engaged.

DAILY READINGS

Twelfth Week, First Day

Then came to him the mother of the sons of Zebedee
with her sons, worshipping him, and asking a certain
thing of him. And he said unto her, What wouldest
thou? She saith unto him, Command that these my two
sons may sit, one on thy right hand, and one on thy
left hand, in thy kingdom. But Jesus answered and
said, Ye know not what ye ask. Are ye able to drink
the cup that I am about to drink? They say unto him,
We are able. He saith unto them, My cup indeed ye
shall drink: but to sit on my right hand, and on my
left hand, is not mine to give, but it is for them for
whom it hath been prepared of my Father. And when
the ten heard it, they were moved with indignation concerning the two brethren. But Jesus called them unto
him, and said, Ye know that the rulers of the Gentiles
lord it over them, and their great ones exercise authority
over them. Not so shall it be among you: but whosoever would become great among you shall be your minister; and whosoever would be first among you shall be
your servant: even as the Son of man came not to be
ministered unto, but to minister, and to give his life a
ransom for many.—Matt. 20: 20-28.

Jesus seems not so much a person as a *universe of*

personality. That is the moral to which our inquiry apparently leads. By *universe* is meant a single whole, which includes everything within itself in a self-consistent unity; and the fact that so many different people discover their own ideal type of personality in Jesus justifies our speaking of Him as a universe of personality. Yet not without one large qualification.

Not every one who has looked upon Jesus has found Him admirable; and in our time there has been one loud and direct challenge to Jesus and the whole view of things that Jesus represents. The name of Nietzsche has been upon everybody's lips now for some years. He is taken to represent the theoretical and philosophical side of the exaggerated national self-consciousness of Germany in the past generation, its worship of power, and its ruthlessness in war. This is not altogether fair to Nietzsche, who would have been the last person to justify the mere worship of massed brute force. Nietzsche's concern was for personality; and because he believed that the Christian doctrine of self-renunciation undermined the foundations of personality, he preached over against it the doctrine of self-assertion.

As a matter of fact, Nietzsche was not without some reason for this attitude. Christianity has too often appeared as a sickly sentimentality, a weak and yielding emotionalism. Its graces of compassion and sympathy have seemed soft and backboneless concessions to weakness. Against this kind of thing Nietzsche loudly and rightly protested. But, like most protesters, he protested too much. He mistook a perversion of the real thing for the real thing itself, and assailed Christianity when he was really assailing a degenerate form of it. He did not discriminate clearly. And there can be no question that this vehement challenge was needed, in order to brace up our conception and practice of the Christian morality.

At the same time, Nietzsche's own philosophical principle is in effect a direct denial of the Christian. He believed it to be possible to produce a type of manhood as much superior to the one we know as the one we know is superior to the highest types of animal life. To this superior type he gave the name of the "superman." But the superman was to grow by the process of self-assertion, by exercising "the will to power"; and in time he would emerge out of this general chaos of self-assertiveness the unchallenged master and lord. So Nietzsche exalts individualism; and the real type of manhood which on this showing proves to be admirable is Napoleon, the masterful, self-assertive, dominant, imperious man.

Now, whether that view is true or untrue, it is, of course, in direct contradiction of Jesus. For, instead of self-assertion, Jesus required self-denial; instead of the "will to power," Jesus preached the "will to love." Nietzsche preached the doctrine of struggle as the process of producing the superman, but Jesus preached the doctrine of cooperation. And not only did He preach, but He also practiced. We know Him as the perfect exemplar of self-denial, and as the living embodiment of the "will to love."

So we may say that the contrast between Napoleon and Jesus sets out the two broad antagonistic views of life. When Professor Cramb looked upon the growing militarization of Europe, he said that Corsica had conquered Galilee; he forgot to add that Corsica ended in St. Helena, and Galilee in an empty grave. But he was right in putting Corsica in antithesis to Galilee. There is no room for the Napoleonic view of life in the philosophy of Jesus. The two are mutually exclusive. So that if we speak of Jesus as a *universe* of personality, it is with the qualification that the Napoleonic type is outside of it. Which represents the true type, whether Jesus or Napoleon is the real superman, it should not be difficult today to decide.

Twelfth Week, Second Day

So that the law hath been our tutor to bring us unto Christ, that we might be justified by faith. But now that faith is come, we are no longer under a tutor. For ye are all sons of God, through faith, in Christ Jesus. For as many of you as were baptized into Christ did put on Christ. There can be neither Jew nor Greek, there can be neither bond nor free, there can be no male and female: for ye all are one man in Christ Jesus.—Gal. 3: 24-28.

Tennyson used to speak of the "man-woman" in Jesus, the singular union in Him of strength and tenderness. The difference of sex is the very deepest and most universal of human distinctions. Yet it would be difficult to discover a single act of Jesus which a woman might not have done. The cleansing of the Temple was less an achievement of physical strength than of moral power; and there have been women in history capable of acts of that kind. We usually ascribe the qualities of initiative and aggressive strength to men, gentleness and the power of endurance to women; and in a general way the distinction is valid. It would puzzle us very much to say which was the more prominent in Jesus. Among His friends were as many women as men, and it is notorious that He has historically spoken with more power to women than to men. Yet no one would dream of suggesting that He was not a true full-blooded man, the embodiment of the ultimate manliness.

This suggests that there was a certain *elemental* quality in the humanity of Jesus, something in it which transcended the difference of sex or temperament, nation or station. It was the simple primal essence of manhood, unqualified and undifferentiated by any of those accidents which divide the man from the woman, the Jew from the Gentile, the king from the peasant, the ancient from the modern. Yet He was a peasant of Galilee. Hailing from an obscure village in an obscure land, born of a people trained through long ages into unparalleled exclusiveness and narrowness, appearing at perhaps the lowest ebb in the history of religion and thought, yet there was a universality in His outlook which bade His disciples go and make disciples of all nations, and a universality of appeal in His manhood which has made and is still making disciples for Him among all the peoples. Reared in an atmosphere which made for the most uncompromising particularism, yet Jesus is the most universal figure in history. This is a point surely worth pursuing farther.

Twelfth Week, Third Day

Wherefore remember, that aforetime ye, the Gentiles in the flesh, who are called Uncircumcision by that which is called Circumcision, in the flesh, made by hands; that ye were at that time separate from Christ, alienated from the commonwealth of Israel, and strangers from the covenants of the promise, having no hope and without God in the world. But now in Christ Jesus ye that once were far off are made nigh in the blood of Christ. For he is our peace, who made both one, and brake down the middle wall of partition, having abolished in his flesh the enmity, even the law of commandments contained in ordinances; that he might create in himself of the twain one new man, so making peace; and might reconcile them both in one body unto God through the cross, having slain the enmity thereby: and he came and preached peace to you that were far off, and peace to them that were nigh: for through him we both have our access in one Spirit unto the Father. So then ye are no more strangers and sojourners, but ye are fellow-citizens with the saints, and of the household of God, being built upon the foundation of the apostles and prophets, Christ Jesus himself being the chief corner stone; in whom each several building, fitly framed together, groweth into a holy temple in the Lord; in whom ye also are builded together for a habitation of God in the Spirit.—Eph. 2: 11-22.

The average Frenchman can never wholly understand Oliver Cromwell any more than the average Englishman can understand John Knox. We should hardly ask a German to say the last word about Joan of Arc or an Italian about Martin Luther. Education and travel and the growth of international feeling have done much to familiarize the nations with each other's heroes. Nevertheless, the factor of *race*[1] still remains an essential condition of the full interpretation of the great historical figures.

But the point can be pushed farther. Not every Englishman can or does understand Oliver Cromwell. It requires an Englishman of a certain type, the man of Puritan inheritance and spirit. It is notorious that the name of Oliver Cromwell still only irritates many of his countrymen. Not the race factor only, but what we may call the temperament factor, counts for something in the understanding of a given person.

There is another step we have to take. The modern Puritan may be able to trace and to appreciate the historical significance of Cromwell's brief but momentous intrusion into English politics. He may be able to analyze Cromwell's mind and character so far as to discover the mainsprings of his actions. But he can never feel that warm immediate sympathy, that intense personal spell which bound Cromwell's men to him as with bands of steel. Times have changed, and with them the temper of society, the religious outlook, the national character. We may study, admire, respect Cromwell, but the most fierce Puritan cannot nowadays get up a genuine personal passion for him. It required a fierce Puritan of his own time to do that; for Cromwell was, as we of ours, a child of his own time. Not only, then, are the race factor and the temperament factor important, but we need also the time factor as a condition of a full understanding of an historical person.

---

[1] By "race" here is not meant a difference of physical inheritance. Nowadays we know that racial and national differences are born chiefly of cultural and social heredity.

But what is true of the understanding of Oliver Cromwell is not true of the understanding of Jesus of Nazareth. He was a Jew, in everything, yet this is almost the last thing we think of concerning Him. He appeals to every race of men without distinction; and our missionary records tell us how the Mongol finds as easy and as many points of contact with Him as a Latin or a Celt. It is probably true that He does not appear quite the same to the Eastern as to the Western eye; but that is due not to any difference in Him, but to the difference in those who look at Him. In His own day, the foreigner found easy access to Him. A Samaritan woman was surprised to find herself speaking intimately with Him. A Roman officer found it easy to approach Him; a Syrophenician woman could not be driven away from Him. Yet the very gait of a Jew of any consequence in those days bade the foreigner keep his distance. When in later days His story went abroad among the nations, first the Greek, then the Roman, then the Teuton and the Celt all capitulated to Him. He appealed to them all—in different ways and at different points, no doubt—but so effectively that they all responded. Compare this with the story of Muhammad. Muhammad has never touched the outer west or the outer east, the farther north or the farther south. His appeal, powerful as in many ways it has been, has nevertheless been comparatively restricted and narrow. But east and west, north and south, Jesus has touched the minds and hearts of men. Even the Muhammadans have made a Muhammadan of Him. He is the one person who seems to be at home anywhere in the world.

Twelfth Week, Fourth Day

Now when Jesus was born in Bethlehem of Judæa in the days of Herod the king, behold, wise men from the east came to Jerusalem, saying, Where is he that is born King of the Jews? for we saw his star in the east, and are come to worship him . . . and lo, the star, which they saw in the east, went before them, till it came and stood over where the young child was. And when they saw the star, they rejoiced with exceeding great joy. And they came into the house and saw the young child with Mary his mother; and they fell down and worshipped him; and opening their treasures they offered unto him gifts, gold and frankincense and myrrh. —Matt. 2: 1, 2, 9-11.

And it came to pass, when the angels went away from them into heaven, the shepherds said one to another, Let us now go even unto Bethlehem, and see this thing that is come to pass, which the Lord hath made known unto us. And they came with haste, and found both Mary and Joseph, and the babe lying in the manger. And when they saw it, they made known concerning the saying which was spoken to them about this child. And all that heard it wondered at the things which were spoken unto them by the shepherds. But Mary kept all these sayings, pondering them in her heart. And the shepherds returned, glorifying and praising God for all the things that they had heard and seen, even as it was spoken unto them.—Luke 2: 15-20.

We have seen the super-national appeal of Jesus. The same quality of universality is to be observed in the matter of temperament. Men of reflection and men of action have sought and found their highest inspiration in Him. The philosopher and the moralist have been compelled to take account of Him. No other single individual has so stimulated the artistic powers—whether in music or in painting; the poet and the social reformer have sat at His feet. He inspires the massive thought of an Augustine and the power of a Luther, the endurance of a Hus and the heroism of a Gordon. The nobleman and the peasant both have bowed to Him. So in His own day, Joseph of Arimathea and Matthew the publican—men at extreme opposite poles of social status —followed Him. The calm, reflective Nathanael and the impetuous Peter found themselves at His feet. All men who came within touching distance of Him found points of contact with Him.

Nor has the appeal of Jesus been confined to a particular age. The whole course of Christian history is studded with those martyrdoms which show how, not only among all races but in all ages, men have been bound to Him by indissoluble ties of loyalty and love. From the Christian slaves who were martyred "to make a Roman holiday" to the Chinese Christians of our day who died rather than repudiate Him, there has been no decline in His personal power over men. He belongs not to one age but to every age. The change which time brings may alter the exact incidence of His appeal, but it abates none of its force. Jesus has never yet been out of date.

The universality of His person is reflected in His outlook upon life and in His teaching. Look, for instance, at His illustrations. The prodigal son is a perennially universal type. The stories of the lost coin, the good Samaritan, the Pharisee and the publican, are for ever true. We know the prodigal and the Samaritan, the Pharisee and the publican, perfectly well. They are here with us today. G. K. Chesterton said a very fine and a very true thing not long ago. Speaking of the principle that self-sacrifice is the way of self-realization, he added, "Jesus said that long ago, as He said almost everything."

Twelfth Week, Fifth Day

Therefore seeing we have this ministry, even as we obtained mercy, we faint not: but we have renounced the hidden things of shame, not walking in craftiness, nor handling the word of God deceitfully; but by the manifestation of the truth commending ourselves to every man's conscience in the sight of God. But and if our gospel is veiled, it is veiled in them that are perishing: in whom the god of this world hath blinded the minds of the unbelieving, that the light of the gospel of the glory of Christ, who is the image of God, should not dawn upon them. For we preach not ourselves, but Christ Jesus as Lord, and ourselves as your servants

for Jesus' sake.   Seeing it is God, that said, Light shall
shine out of darkness, who shined in our hearts, to give
the light of the knowledge of the glory of God in the
face of Jesus Christ.—II Cor. 4: 1-6.

In one of his letters Dostoievsky speaks of "the inmost
essence and the ultimate destiny of the Russian nation
—namely, that Russia must reveal to the world her own
Russian Christ, whom as yet the people know not."
And he adds: "There lies, I believe, the inmost essence
of our vast impending contribution to civilization, where-
by we shall awaken the European people; there lies the
inmost core of our exuberant and intense existence that
is to be." It may be that, when the present confusion
and unrest have been allayed and Russia is once more
at peace with herself and with mankind, she will achieve
her own vision of Christ and reveal it to the world.

But it is not Russia alone which has a Christ to reveal.
We have seen how Jesus has appealed to the nations of
men; and Russia and all the other nations will each see
Him in their own way. And it is when He is seen of
all the nations, and every nation in the light of its
own peculiar history and discipline and genius shows its
own Christ to the world, that we shall have the finished
picture of "the Christ that is to be."

That is, of course, if the picture can ever be finished.
St. Paul speaks of "the unsearchable riches of Christ";
and if it be true that in Him "are all the treasures of
wisdom and knowledge hidden," then it may well be that
the picture of Christ will never be quite complete until
we see Him as He is. Some new phase of His significance, some unsuspected element in His personality, will
be continually revealed to us; and, indeed, as "knowledge
grows from more to more," it would be strange if we did
not identify in Him some new treasure of "the manifold
wisdom of God."

But shall we ever outgrow Jesus? Will there ever be
a time when the revelation of God in Jesus will be itself

transcended, as it transcended Judaism? He would indeed be a rash person who presumed that he knew the whole counsel of God so well as to say that God has no resources of revelation beyond those He has given us in Jesus. At the same time, a question of this kind is not particularly useful. When mankind has reached the moral plane of Jesus, it will be time enough to look out for fresh revelations. The exhaustion of the significance of Jesus is yet a very remote possibility; and it is our business to explore the continent which lies at our feet, rather than speculate about the probabilities on the other side of it. In the present state of human development, Jesus is still a universe in which there is much unknown territory to be explored and much land to be possessed. And when Russia has revealed to the world her Russian Christ, and India her own Indian Christ, and China her own Chinese Christ, and when the islands of the sea tell their tale of what they have found Christ to be, we shall know better what was and is "the light of the knowledge of the glory of God in the face of Jesus Christ." And even then, we shall not have got the tale complete.

Twelfth Week, Sixth Day

As therefore ye received Christ Jesus the Lord, so walk in him, rooted and builded up in him, and stablished in your faith, even as ye were taught, abounding in thanksgiving.
Take heed lest there shall be any one that maketh spoil of you through his philosophy and vain deceit, after the tradition of men, after the rudiments of the world, and not after Christ: for in him dwelleth all the fulness of the Godhead bodily, and in him ye are made full.—Col. 2: 6-10.

It may be said that there are four main strands in the total impression which Jesus has made upon men:

First, as the Good Shepherd, the embodiment of love

and faithfulness and care—*the symbol of a friendly providence.*

Second, as the Man of Sorrows, whom it pleased the Lord to bruise and upon whom were laid the transgressions of His people, the Lamb of God who taketh away the sin of the world—*the symbol of redemption.*

Third, as the Light of the World, the clue to the mystery of the universe, the key to the problems of life—*the symbol of illumination.*

Fourth, as the Carpenter of Nazareth, who shared the common lot and toil of men, who was made in all things like unto His brethren—*the symbol of common humanity.*

Between these aspects under which men have seen Jesus there is no contradiction, for each of them corresponds to a definite human need. There are times when, in its loneliness and bewilderment, the soul cries out for the Good Shepherd who will go out to it into the wilderness and carry it home on His shoulders rejoicing. There are other times when the soul, distracted and desperate by reason of its moral defeats and failures, calls out for a Redeemer who will deliver it from its body of death. There are also times when the mind is perplexed and overwhelmed by the mystery of things, by the contradictions of life, by the vexing challenge of thought and knowledge; and then it asks for light. And in the long historic struggle for the great human sanctities and liberties, men have turned for endorsement, courage, and inspiration to the Carpenter of Nazareth.

And all these various aspects must be gathered up into a complete picture of Jesus. St. Paul speaks of "the manifold wisdom of God"; and this word *manifold* may be translated "many-colored." He is speaking of God's self-revelation in Jesus Christ, and when the white light of this revelation is refracted by the prism of human need it breaks up into these various ministries of deliverance and enlightenment, providence and inspiration. It is only as we rightly appraise all these ministries and try to unify them in a single picture, that we shall behold that glory which was "as of the only begotten from the Father."

Twelfth Week, Seventh Day

My soul doth magnify the Lord,
And my spirit hath rejoiced in God my Saviour.
For he hath looked upon the low estate of his hand-
    maiden:
For behold, from henceforth all generations shall call
    me blessed.
For he that is mighty hath done to me great things;
And holy is his name.
And his mercy is unto generations and generations
On them that fear him.
He hath shewed strength with his arm;
He hath scattered the proud in the imagination of their
    heart.
He hath put down princes from their thrones,
And hath exalted them of low degree.
The hungry he hath filled with good things;
And the rich he hath sent empty away.
He hath holpen Israel his servant,
That he might remember mercy
(As he spake unto our fathers)
Toward Abraham and his seed for ever.—Luke 1: 46-55.

It is not only the need of the single soul that changes with the passing of time, but the need of the collective soul—the need of the age; and every age will tend to give prominence to that aspect of Christ that fits its own peculiar need. We have seen how the painters of the Renascence emphasized the redeeming grace of Jesus, and this was the ruling element in the spiritual experience of the Reformation period. This was, no doubt, due to the circumstance that the soul, having emancipated itself from its subjection to an all-embracing spiritual authority, became aware in a new, vivid way of its own direct moral responsibility and of its incapacity to discharge this responsibility in its own strength. Being thus acutely conscious of the meaning of its moral defeats and falls, it began to crave a redeemer, and this redeemer it found in Jesus. Every age will see Jesus in terms of its own peculiar need.

And so must ours. What is the need of our age? Truly our age gathers up into its own need the whole manifold need of all the ages; and it will need a whole Christ to see it through its troubles. But, specially, the task of our age is the fulfilment of the democratic ideal.

The democratic principle rests upon the doctrine of the infinite and therefore the equal worth of every living soul, and, though we may not say that this doctrine originated with Christianity, it is true that it has derived its most powerful impulse from Christianity; and it is not alone a political task but a definitely Christian task to carry out the logic of this principle—which is to establish within the commonwealth those conditions of equal opportunity which are within human control.

We have passed from that state of the world when the divine right of kings kept common men out of their inheritance of life and liberty, and we are going to build a new world upon the principle that every man is a king by divine right. But we learned that principle from the vision of the Carpenter of Nazareth.

We sometimes describe the Incarnation as God coming down to our human level. That, however, is only half the truth. The other half is that God raised our humanity up to His own plane. One of the old Fathers speaks of our flesh being gathered up into the Godhead. And we shall create a democratic world only as we learn to conceive and to interpret humanity in this way—as we realize that, when God took upon Him the flesh of a common man, He touched the common man with divinity for evermore.

Somewhere within this cycle there is a vision of Jesus awaiting this generation; and, when we see it, we shall understand how inevitable it was that the Son of God should be also the Son of Man.

SUGGESTIONS FOR THOUGHT AND DISCUSSION

Does the fact that the appeal of Jesus is so universal suggest that human nature is always and everywhere the same?

What light does this week's reading throw upon the missionary and social obligation of the Church?

It has been said that "democracy is Christianity in public affairs." Is this true? Is democracy as we know it truly Christian? If not, what does it need in order to make it so?

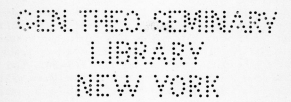